The Gene Edwards Signature Collection

* * *

A Tale of Three Kings

The Prisoner in the Third Cell

The Divine Romance

THE *Gene Edwards* SIGNATURE COLLECTION

A Tale of Three Kings

The Prisoner in the Third Cell

The Divine Romance

Visit Tyndale online at tyndale.com.

Visit Tyndale Momentum online at tyndalemomentum.com.

TYNDALE, Tyndale's quill logo, *Tyndale Momentum*, and the Tyndale Momentum logo are registered trademarks of Tyndale House Ministries. Tyndale Momentum is the nonfiction imprint of Tyndale House Publishers, Carol Stream, Illinois.

The Gene Edwards Signature Collection: A Tale of Three Kings, The Prisoner in the Third Cell, The Divine Romance

A Tale of Three Kings was previously published in 1980 and 1992 by Tyndale House Publishers under ISBN 978-0-8423-6908-4 and by SeedSowers (Christian Books Publishing House), Newnan, Georgia 30263.

The Prisoner in the Third Cell was previously published in 1991 by Tyndale House Publishers under ISBN 978-0-8423-5023-5 and by SeedSowers (Christian Books Publishing House), Auburn, Maine 04210.

The Divine Romance was previously published in 1984 and 1992 by Tyndale House Publishers under ISBN 978-0-8423-1092-5 and by SeedSowers (Christian Books Publishing House), Auburn, Maine 04210.

Designed by Lindy Martin at Faceout Studios

For information about special discounts for bulk purchases, please contact Tyndale House Publishers at csresponse@tyndale.com, or call 1-800-323-9400.

ISBN 978-1-4964-5103-3

Printed in the United States of America

27 26 25 24 23 22 21
7 6 5 4 3 2 1

Contents

* * *

A TALE OF THREE KINGS

To the brokenhearted Christians
coming out of authoritarian groups, seeking solace,
healing, and hope. May you somehow recover
and go on with him who is liberty.
And to all brokenhearted Christians:
May you be so utterly healed that you can still answer
the call of him who asks for all because he is all.

And to Helen, Carman, and Patty for aiding in the preparation of this manuscript.

* * *

Preface

WHEN I FIRST PENNED *A Tale of Three Kings*, I would have been encouraged to know it would live long enough to go through two or three printings. I utterly underestimated the number of devastated Christians out there. A far broader audience than I anticipated has taken up this book. It is an audience made up of Christians damaged by such things as church splits and individual "Christian to Christian" clashes.

I have been a little awed by the reception of this book and the fact that the reception has been worldwide. The number of Christian workers who have ordered this book in bulk, to be passed out to their people, has been only short of phenomenal. That *A Tale of Three Kings* has been turned into plays and has been read publicly from pulpits turned awe to amazement.

Obviously, there is a great deal of pain and hurt out there in Christendom that is rarely addressed or ministered to. I hope this book, as well as *Letters to a Devastated Christian*, *Crucified by Christians*, and *The Prisoner in the Third Cell*, will minister to those needs.

Author's Note

WHY THIS BOOK AND WHAT IS ITS PURPOSE? The answer can probably be traced to my mailbox. As one who receives correspondence from Christians all over the world, I noted some years ago a growing number of letters from Christians devastated by the authoritarian movement that had become so popular with many evangelical groups. A reaction to this totalitarian concept eventually set in. A mass exodus was soon under way. The stories being told by these spiritual fugitives are often terrifying and sometimes unbelievable. I am not at all sure if it is the doctrine itself that is causing such widespread carnage or the inordinate practice of this doctrine. Whatever it is, in all my long years as an evangelical Christian minister, I have never seen anything that has damaged so many believers so deeply. The wreckage appears to be universal, and recovery from it is almost nil.

This book reflects my concern for this multitude of confused, brokenhearted, and often bitter Christians who now find their spiritual lives in shambles and who are groping about for even the slightest word of hope and comfort.

This book, I trust, will serve in some small way to meet this need.

There is one thing, dear reader, this book is most certainly not intended to be. It is not intended to be additional fodder in your cannon to better blast your adversaries, whatever your view. I would beg you to be done with such ancient and brutish ways. This book is intended for individual healing and for private retreat.

I trust this volume will sound a note of hope, even if that note is heard ever so distantly.

Gene Edwards

They have set up kings,
but not by me:
they have made princes,
and I knew it not . . .
HOSEA 8:4

* * *

Well, dear reader, how nice to be with you once more. It is a privilege to spend this time with you. Thank you for meeting here, and I suggest we hasten into the playhouse, as I see that they have already dimmed the lights.

There are two seats reserved for us not too far from the stage. Quickly, let us take them.

I understand the story is a drama. I trust, though, you will not find it sad.

I believe we will find the story to be in two parts. In part 1 we shall meet an older king, Saul by name, and a young shepherd boy named David. In part 2 we shall once more meet an older king and a young man. But this time the older king is David and the young man is Absalom.

The story is a portrait (you might prefer to call it a rough charcoal sketch) of submission and authority within the kingdom of God.

Ah, they have turned off the lights, and the players have taken their places. The audience has quieted itself. The curtain is rising.

Our story has begun.

Prologue

THE ALMIGHTY, LIVING GOD TURNED to Gabriel and gave a command.

"Go, take these two portions of my being. There are two destinies waiting. To each unborn destiny give one portion of myself."

Carrying two glowing, pulsating lights of Life, Gabriel opened the door into the realm between two universes and disappeared. He had stepped into the Mall of Unborn Destinies.

Gabriel spoke: "I have here two portions of the nature of God. The first is the very cloth of his nature. When wrapped about you, it clothes you with the breath of God. As water surrounds a person in the sea, so will his very breath envelop you. With this, *the divine breath,* you will have his power–power to subdue armies, shame the enemies of God, and accomplish his work on the earth. Here is the power of God as a gift. Here is immersion into the Spirit."

A destiny stepped forward: "This portion of God is for me."

"True," replied the angel. "And remember, whoever receives such a great portion of power will surely be known by many. Ere your earthly pilgrimage is done, your true character will be known; yea, it will be *revealed* by means of this power. Such is the destiny of all who want and wield this portion, for it touches only the outer person, affecting the inner person not one whit. Outer power will always unveil the inner resources or the lack thereof."

The first destined one received the gift and stepped back.

Gabriel spoke again.

"I have here the second of two elements of the living God. This is not a gift but an inheritance. A gift is worn on the outer person; an inheritance is planted deep inside–like a seed. Yet, even though it is such a small planting, this planting grows and, in time, fills all the inner person."

Another destiny stepped forward. "I believe this element is to be mine for my earthly pilgrimage."

"True," responded the angel again. "I must tell you that what has been given to you is a glorious thing–the only element in the universe that can change the human heart. Yet even this element of God cannot accomplish its task nor grow and fill your entire inner being unless it is compounded well. It must be mixed lavishly with pain, sorrow, and crushing."

The second destined one received the inheritance and stepped back.

Beside Gabriel sat the angel Recorder. He dutifully entered into his ledger the record of the two destinies.

"And who shall these destinies become after they go through the door to the visible universe?" asked Recorder.

Gabriel replied softly, "Each, in his time, shall be king."

PART 1

CHAPTER 1

THE YOUNGEST SON OF ANY FAMILY bears two distinctions: He is considered to be both spoiled and uninformed. Usually little is expected of him. Inevitably, he displays fewer characteristics of leadership than the other children in the family. As a child, he never leads. He only follows, for he has no one younger on whom to practice leadership.

So it is today. And so it was three thousand years ago in a village called Bethlehem, in a family of eight boys. The first seven sons of Jesse worked near their father's farm. The youngest was sent on treks into the mountains to graze the family's small flock of sheep.

On those pastoral jaunts, this youngest son always carried two things: a sling and a small, guitarlike instrument. Spare time for a sheepherder is abundant on rich mountain plateaus where sheep can graze for days in one sequestered meadow. But as time passed and days became weeks, the young man became very lonely. The feeling of friendlessness that always roamed inside him was magnified.

He often cried. He also played his harp a great deal. He had a good voice, so he often sang. When these activities failed to comfort him, he gathered up a pile of stones and, one by one, swung them at a distant tree with something akin to fury.

When one rock pile was depleted, he would walk to the blistered tree, reassemble his rocks, and designate another leafy enemy at yet a farther distance.

He engaged in many such solitary battles.

This shepherd-singer-slinger also loved his Lord. At night, when all the sheep lay sleeping and he sat staring at the dying fire, he would strum upon his harp and break into quiet song. He sang the ancient hymns of his forefathers' faith. While he sang he wept, and while weeping he often broke out in abandoned praise–until mountains in distant places lifted up his praise and tears and passed them on to higher mountains, until they eventually reached the ears of God.

When the young shepherd did not praise and when he did not cry, he tended to each and every sheep and lamb. When not occupied with his flock, he swung his companionable sling and swung it again and again until he could tell every rock precisely where to go.

Once, while singing his lungs out to God, angels, sheep, and passing clouds, he spied a living enemy: a huge bear! He lunged forward. Both found themselves moving furiously toward the same small object, a lamb feeding at a table of rich, green grass. Youth and bear stopped halfway and whirled to face one another. Even as he instinctively reached into his pocket for a stone, the young man realized, "Why, I am not afraid."

Meanwhile, brown lightning on mighty, furry legs charged at the shepherd with foaming madness. Impelled by the strength of youth, the young man married rock to leather, and soon a brook-smooth pebble whined through the air to meet that charge.

A few moments later, the man–not quite so young as a moment before–picked up the little lamb and said, "I am your shepherd, and God is mine."

And so, long into the night, he wove the day's saga into a song. He hurled that hymn to the skies again and again until he had taught the melody and words to every angel that had ears. They, in turn, became custodians of this wondrous song and passed it on as healing balm to brokenhearted men and women in every age to come.

CHAPTER 2

A FIGURE IN THE DISTANCE WAS running toward him. It grew and became his brother. "Run!" cried the brother. "Run with all your strength. I'll watch the flock."

"Why?"

"An old man, a sage. He wants to meet all eight of the sons of Jesse, and he has seen all but you."

"But why?"

"Run!"

So David ran. He stopped long enough to get his breath. Then, sweat pouring down his sunburned cheeks, his red face matching his red curly hair, he walked into his father's house, his eyes recording everything in sight.

The youngest son of Jesse stood there, tall and strong, but more in the eyes of the curious old gentleman than to anyone else in the room. Kith and kin cannot always tell when a man is grown, even when looking straight at him. The elderly man saw. And something more he saw. In a way he himself did not understand, the old man knew what God knew.

God had taken a house-to-house survey of the whole kingdom in search of someone very special. As a result of this survey, the Lord God Almighty had found that this leather-lunged troubadour loved his Lord with a purer heart than anyone else on all the sacred soil of Israel.

"Kneel," said the bearded one with the long, gray hair. Almost regally, for one who had never been in that particular position, David knelt and then felt oil pouring down on his head. Somewhere, in one of the closets of his mind labeled "childhood information," he found a thought: *This is what men do to designate royalty! Samuel is making me a . . . what?*

The Hebrew words were unmistakable. Even children knew them.

"Behold the Lord's anointed!"

Quite a day for that young man, wouldn't you say? Then do you find it strange that this remarkable event led the young man not to the throne but to a decade of hellish agony and suffering? On that day, David was enrolled, not into the lineage of royalty but into the school of brokenness.

Samuel went home. The sons of Jesse, save one, went forth to war. And the youngest, not yet ripe for war, received a promotion in his father's home . . . from sheepherder to messenger boy. His new job was to run food and messages to his brothers on the front lines. He did this regularly.

On one such visit to the battlefront, he killed another bear, in exactly the same way as he had the first. This bear, however, was nine feet tall and bore the name Goliath. As a result of this unusual feat, young David found himself a folk hero.

And eventually he found himself in the palace of a mad king. And in circumstances that were as insane as the king, the young man was to learn many indispensable lessons.

CHAPTER 3

DAVID SANG TO THE MAD KING. Often. The music helped the old man a great deal, it seems. And all over the palace, when David sang, everyone stopped in the corridors, turned their ears in the direction of the king's chamber, and listened and wondered. How did such a young man come to possess such wonderful words and music?

Everyone's favorite seemed to be the song the little lamb had taught him. They loved that song as much as did the angels.

Nonetheless, the king was mad, and therefore he was jealous. Or was it the other way around? Either way, Saul felt threatened by David, as kings often do when there is a popular, promising young man beneath them. The king also knew, as did David, that this boy just might have his job some day.

But would David ascend to the throne by fair means or foul? Saul did not know. This question is one of the things that drove the king mad.

David was caught in a very uncomfortable position; however, he seemed to grasp a deep understanding of the unfolding drama in which he had been caught. He seemed to understand something that few of even the wisest men of his day understood. Something that in our day, when men are wiser still, even fewer understand.

And what was that?

God did not have–but wanted very much to have–men and women who would live in pain.

God wanted a broken vessel.

CHAPTER 4

THE MAD KING SAW DAVID AS a threat to the *king's* kingdom. Saul did not understand, it seems, that God should be left to decide what kingdoms survive which threats. Not knowing this, Saul did what all mad kings do. He threw spears at David. He could. He was *king.* Kings can do things like that. They almost always do. Kings claim the right to throw spears. Everyone knows that kings have that right. Everyone knows very, very well. How do they know? Because the king has told them so–many, many times.

Is it possible that this mad king was the *true* king, even the Lord's anointed?

And what about your king? Is he the Lord's anointed? Maybe he is. Maybe he isn't. No one can ever really know for sure. Men say they are sure. Even *certain.* But they are not. They do not know. God knows. But he will not tell.

If your king is truly the Lord's anointed, and if he also *throws spears,* then there are some things you *can* know, and know for sure:

Your king is quite mad.

And he is a king after the order of King Saul.

CHAPTER 5

GOD HAS A UNIVERSITY. It's a small school. Few enroll; even fewer graduate. Very, very few indeed.

God has this school because he does not have broken men and women. Instead, he has several other types of people. He has people who claim to have God's authority . . . and don't–people who claim to be broken . . . and aren't. And people who *do have* God's authority, but who are mad *and* unbroken. And he has, regretfully, a great mixture of everything in between. All of these he has in abundance, but broken men and women, hardly at all.

In God's sacred school of submission and brokenness, why are there so few students? Because all students in this school must suffer much pain. And as you might guess, it is often the unbroken ruler (whom God sovereignly picks) who metes out the pain. David was once a student in this school, and Saul was God's chosen way to crush David.

As the king grew in madness, David grew in understanding.

He knew that God had placed him in the king's palace under true authority.

The authority of King Saul was *true*? Yes, God's chosen authority. *Chosen for David.* Unbroken authority, yes. But divine in ordination, nonetheless.

Yes, that is possible.

David drew in his breath, placed himself under his mad king, and moved farther down the path of his earthly hell.

CHAPTER 6

DAVID HAD A QUESTION: What do you do when someone throws a spear at you?

Does it seem odd to you that David did not know the answer to this question? After all, everyone else in the world knows what to do when a spear is thrown at you. Why, you pick up the spear and throw it right back!

"When someone throws a spear at you, David, just wrench it out of the wall and throw it back. Everyone else does, you can be sure."

And in performing this small feat of returning thrown spears, you will prove many things: You are courageous. You stand for the right. You boldly stand against the wrong. You are tough and can't be pushed around. You will not stand for injustice or unfair treatment. You are the defender of the faith, keeper of the flame, detector of all heresy. You will not be wronged. All of these attributes then combine to prove that you are also a candidate for kingship. Yes, perhaps *you* are the Lord's anointed.

After the order of King Saul.

There is also a possibility that some twenty years after your coronation, you will be the most incredibly skilled spear thrower in all the realm. And also by then . . .

Quite mad.

CHAPTER 7

UNLIKE ANYONE ELSE IN spear-throwing history, David did *not* know what to do when a spear was thrown at him. He did not throw Saul's spears back at him. Nor did he make any spears of his own and throw them. Something was different about David. All he did was dodge the spears.

What can a man, especially a young man, do when the king decides to use him for target practice? What if the young man decides not to return the compliment?

First of all, he must pretend he cannot see spears. Even when they are coming straight at him. Second, he must learn to duck very quickly. Last, he must pretend nothing happened.

You can easily tell when someone has been hit by a spear. He turns a deep shade of bitter. David never got hit. Gradually, he learned a very well-kept secret. He discovered three things that prevented him from ever being hit.

One, never learn anything about the fashionable, easily mastered art of spear throwing. Two, stay out of the company of all spear throwers. And three, keep your mouth tightly closed.

In this way, spears will never touch you, even when they pierce your heart.

CHAPTER 8

"MY KING IS MAD. At least, I so perceive him. What can I do?"

First, recognize this immutable fact: You cannot tell (none of us can) who is the Lord's anointed and who is not. Some kings, whom all agree are after the order of King Saul, are really after the order of David. And others, whom all agree are after the order of David, really belong to the order of King Saul. Who is correct? Who can know? To whose voice do you listen? *No man* is wise enough ever to break that riddle. All we can do is walk around asking ourselves this question:

"Is this man the Lord's anointed? And if he is, is he after the order of King Saul?"

Memorize that question very well. You may have to ask it of yourself ten thousand times. Especially if you are a citizen of a realm whose king just might be mad.

Asking this question may not seem difficult, but it is. Especially when you are crying very hard . . . and dodging spears . . . and being tempted to throw one back . . . and being encouraged by others to do just that. And all your rationality and sanity and logic and intelligence and common sense agree. But in the midst of your tears and your frustration, remember that you know only the question, not the answer.

No one knows the answer.

Except God.

And he *never* tells.

CHAPTER 9

"I DID NOT LIKE THAT LAST CHAPTER. It skirted the problem. I'm in David's situation, and I am in agony. What do I do when the kingdom I'm in is ruled by a spear-wielding king? Should I leave? If so, how? Just what does a person *do* in the middle of a spear-throwing contest?"

Well, if you didn't like the *question* found in the last chapter, you won't like the *answer* found in this one.

The answer is "You get stabbed to death."

"But what is the good in being speared?"

You have your eyes on the wrong King Saul. As long as you look at your king, you will blame him, and him alone, for your present hell. But be careful, for God has *his* eyes fastened sharply on another King Saul. Not the visible one standing up there throwing spears at you. No, God is looking at *another* King Saul. One just as bad–or worse.

God is looking at the King Saul in *you.*

"In *me*?!"

Saul is in your bloodstream, in the marrow of your bones. He makes up the very flesh and muscle of your heart. He is mixed into your soul. He inhabits the nuclei of your atoms.

King Saul is one with you.

You are King Saul!

He breathes in the lungs and beats in the breast of all of us. There is only one way to get rid of him. He must be annihilated.

You may not find this to be a compliment, but at least now you know why God put you under someone who just might be King Saul.

David the sheepherder would have grown up to become King Saul II, except that God cut away the Saul inside David's heart. That operation, by the way, took years and was a brutalizing experience that almost killed the patient.

And what were the scalpel and tongs God used to remove this inner Saul? God used the outer Saul.

King Saul sought to destroy David, but his only success was that he became the instrument of God to put to death the Saul who roamed about in the caverns of David's own soul. Yes, David was virtually destroyed in the process, but this had to be. Otherwise the Saul in him would have survived.

David accepted this fate. He embraced the cruel circumstances. He lifted no hand nor offered resistance. Nor did he grandstand his piety. Silently, privately, he bore the crucible of humiliation. Because of this he was deeply wounded. His whole inner being was mutilated. His personality was altered. When the gore was over, David was barely recognizable.

You weren't satisfied with the question in the last chapter? Then you probably didn't like the answer in this one.

None of us do.

Except God.

CHAPTER 10

HOW DOES A PERSON KNOW WHEN IT is finally time to leave the Lord's anointed–especially if the Lord's anointed is after the order of King Saul?

David never made that decision. The Lord's anointed made it for him. The king's own decree settled the matter!

"Hunt him down; kill him like a dog."

Only then did David leave. No, he fled. Even then, he never spoke a word or lifted a hand against Saul. And please note this: David did not split the kingdom when he made his departure. He did not take part of the population with him. He left *alone.*

Alone. *All* alone. King Saul II never does that. He always takes those who "insist on coming along."

Yes, people do insist on going with you, don't they? They are willing to help you found the kingdom of King Saul II.

Such men *never* dare leave alone.

But David left alone. You see, the Lord's true anointed can leave alone.

There's only *one* way to leave a kingdom:

Alone.

All alone.

CHAPTER 11

CAVES ARE NOT THE IDEAL PLACE for morale building. There is a certain sameness to them all, no matter how many you have lived in. Dark. Wet. Cold. Stale. A cave becomes even worse when you are its sole inhabitant . . . and in the distance you can hear the dogs baying.

But sometimes, when the dogs and hunters were not near, the hunted sang. He started low, then lifted his voice and sang the song the little lamb had taught him. The cavern walls echoed each note just as the mountains had once done. The music rolled down into deep cavern darkness that soon became an echoing choir singing back to him.

He had less now than when he was a shepherd, for now he had no lyre, no sun, not even the company of sheep. The memories of the court had faded. David's greatest ambition now reached no higher than a shepherd's staff. *Everything* was being crushed out of him.

He sang a great deal.

And matched each note with a tear.

How strange, is it not, what suffering begets?

There in those caves, drowned in the sorrow of his song and in the song of his sorrow, David became the greatest hymn writer and the greatest comforter of broken hearts this world shall ever know.

CHAPTER 12

HE RAN—THROUGH SOGGY FIELDS and down slimy riverbeds. Sometimes the dogs came close; sometimes they even *found* him. But swift feet, rivers, and watery pits hid him. He took his food from the fields, dug roots from the roadside, slept in trees, hid in ditches, crawled through briars and mud. For days he ran–not daring to stop or eat. He drank the rain. Half naked, all filthy, on he walked, stumbled, crawled, and clawed.

Caves were castles now. Pits were home.

In times past, mothers had always told their children that if they did not behave they would end up like the town drunk. No longer. They had a better, more frightening story. "Be good, or you'll end up like the giant killer."

In Jerusalem, when teachers taught students to be submissive to the king and to honor the Lord's anointed, David was the parable. "See, this is what God does to rebellious men." The young listeners shuddered at the thought and somberly resolved never to have anything to do with rebellion.

So it was then, so it is now, and so it shall ever be.

Much later, David would reach a foreign land and a small–very small–measure of safety. Here, too, he was feared, hated, lied about, and plotted against. He shook hands with murder on several occasions.

These were David's darkest hours. We know them as his pre-king days, but he didn't. He may have assumed this was his lot forever.

Suffering was giving birth. Humility was being born.

By earthly measures he was a shattered man; by heaven's measure, a broken one.

CHAPTER 13

OTHERS HAD TO FLEE AS THE king's madness grew. First one, then three, then ten, and eventually hundreds. After long searching, some of these fugitives made contact with David. They had not seen him for a long time.

The truth was that when they did see him, they didn't recognize him. He had changed. His personality, his disposition, his total being had been altered. He talked less. He loved God more. He sang differently. They had never heard these songs before. Some were lovely beyond words, but some could freeze the blood in your veins.

Those who found him and decided to be his fellow fugitives were a sorry, worthless lot: thieves, liars, complainers, fault-finders, rebellious men with rebellious hearts. They were blind with hate for the king and, therefore, for all authority figures. They would have been troublemakers in paradise, if ever they could have gotten in.

David did not lead them. He did not share their attitudes. Yet, unsolicited, they began to follow him.

He never spoke to them of authority. He never spoke of submission. But every one of them submitted. He laid down no rules. *Legalism* is not a word found in the vocabulary of fugitives. Nonetheless, they cleaned up their outward lives. Gradually, their inward lives began to change, too.

They didn't fear submission or authority. They didn't even think about the topic, much less discuss it. Then why did they follow him? They didn't, exactly. It was just that he was . . . well . . . David. That didn't need explanation.

And so, for the first time, true kingship had its nativity.

CHAPTER 14

"WHY, DAVID, WHY?"

The place was another nameless cave.

The men stirred about restlessly. Gradually, and very uneasily, they began to settle in. All were as confused as Joab, who had finally voiced their questions.

Joab wanted some answers. Now!

David should have seemed embarrassed or at least defensive. He was neither. He was looking past Joab like a man viewing another realm that only he could see.

Joab walked directly in front of David, looked down on him, and began roaring his frustrations.

"Many times he almost speared you to death in his palace. I saw that with my own eyes. Finally, you ran away. Now for years you have been nothing but a rabbit for him to chase. Furthermore, the whole world believes the lies he tells about you. He has come–the king himself–hunting every cave, pit, and hole on earth to find you and kill you like a dog. But tonight *you* had *him* at the end of his own spear and you did nothing!

"Look at us. We're animals again. Less than an hour ago you could have freed us all. Yes, we could all be free, right now! Free! And Israel, too. She would be free. Why, David? Why did you not end these years of misery?"

There was a long silence. Men shifted again, uneasily. They were not accustomed to seeing David rebuked.

"Because," said David very slowly (and with a gentleness that seemed to say, I heard what you asked, but not the way you asked it), "because once, long ago, he was not mad. He was young. He was great. Great in the eyes of God and men. And it was God who made him king–God–not men."

Joab blazed back, "But now he is *mad*! And God is no longer with him. And David, he will yet kill you!"

This time it was David's answer that blazed with fire.

"Better he kill me than I learn his ways. Better he kill me than I become as he is. I shall not practice the ways that cause kings to go mad. I will not throw spears, nor will I allow hatred to grow in my heart. I will not avenge. I will not destroy the Lord's anointed. Not now. Not ever!"

Joab could not handle such a senseless answer. He stormed out into the dark.

That night men went to bed on cold, wet stone and muttered about their leader's distorted, masochistic views of relationships to kings–especially mad ones.

Angels went to bed that night, too, and dreamed, in the afterglow of that rare, rare day, that God might yet be able to give his authority to a trustworthy vessel.

CHAPTER 15

WHAT KIND OF MAN WAS SAUL? Who was this one who made himself David's enemy? Anointed of God. Deliverer of Israel. And yet remembered mostly for his madness.

Forget the bad press. Forget the stinging reviews. Forget his reputation. Look at the facts. Saul was one of the greatest figures of human history. He was a farm boy, a country kid who made good. He was tall, good-looking, and well-liked.

He was baptized into the Spirit of God.

He also came from a good family. In his lineage were some of the greatest historical figures of all humanity. Abraham, Jacob, Moses–these were his ancestors.

Do you remember the background? Abraham had founded a nation. Moses had set that nation free from slavery. Joshua gave those people a toehold in the land that God had promised them. The judges kept the whole thing from disintegrating into total chaos.

That's when Saul came along. It was Saul who took these people and welded them into a united kingdom.

Saul united a people and founded a kingdom. Few men have ever done that. He created an army out of thin air. He won battles in the power of God, defeated the enemy again and again, as few men have ever done. Remember that, and remember that this man was immersed in the Spirit. Furthermore, he was a prophet. The Spirit came on him in power and authority. He did and said unprecedented things, and it was all by the power of the Spirit resting on him.

He was everything people today are seeking to be . . . empowered with the Holy Spirit . . . able to do the impossible . . . for God. A leader, chosen by God with power from God.

Saul was given authority that is God's alone. He was God's anointed, and God treated him that way.

He was also eaten with jealousy, filled with self-importance, and willing to live in spiritual darkness.

Is there a moral in these contradictions? Yes, and it will splinter a lot of your concepts about power, about great men and women under God's anointing, and about God himself.

Many pray for the power of God. More every year. Those prayers sound powerful, sincere, godly, and without ulterior motive. Hidden under such prayer and fervor, however, are ambition, a craving for fame, the desire to be considered a spiritual giant. The person who prays such a prayer may not even know it, but dark motives and desires are in his heart . . . in *your* heart.

Even as people pray these prayers, they are hollow inside. There is little internal spiritual growth. Prayer for power is the quick and the short way, circumnavigating internal growth.

There is a vast difference between the outward clothing of the Spirit's power and the inward filling of the Spirit's life. In the first, despite the power, the hidden man of the heart may remain unchanged. In the latter, that monster is dealt with.

Interesting about God. He hears all those requests for power, which fervent young men and women pray (in every generation), and he answers them! Very often he grants these requests for power, for authority. Sometimes, in answering them, he says yes to some very unworthy vessels.

He gives unworthy people his power? Even though they are a pile of dead men's bones inside?

Why does God do such a thing? The answer is both simple and shocking. He sometimes gives unworthy vessels a greater portion of power so that others will eventually see the *true* state of internal nakedness within that individual.

So think again when you hear the power merchant. Remember, God sometimes gives power to people for unseen reasons. A person can be living in the grossest of sin, and the outer gift will still be working perfectly. The gifts of God, once given, cannot be recalled. Even in the presence of sin. Furthermore, some people, living just such lives, *are* the Lord's anointed . . . in the Lord's eyes. Saul was living proof of this fact.

The gifts cannot be revoked. Terrifying, isn't it?

If you are young and have never seen such things, you may be certain that sometime in the next forty years you will see. Highly gifted and very powerful men and women . . . reputed to be leaders in the kingdom of God, do some very dark and ugly deeds.

What does this world need: gifted men and women, outwardly empowered? Or individuals who are broken, inwardly transformed?

Keep in mind that some who have been given the very power of God have raised armies, defeated the enemy, brought forth mighty works of God, preached and prophesied with unparalleled power and eloquence . . .

And thrown spears,
And hated other people,
And attacked others,
And plotted to kill,
And prophesied naked,
And even consulted witches.

CHAPTER 16

"YOU STILL HAVEN'T ANSWERED my question. The man I sit under: I think he is a King Saul. How can I know with certainty?"

It is not given to us to know. And remember, even Sauls are often the Lord's anointed.

You see, there are always people–everywhere, in every age, and in every group–who will stand and tell you: "That man is after the order of King Saul." While another, just as sure, will rise to declare, "No, he is the Lord's anointed after the order of David." No one can *really* know which of the two is correct. And if you happen to be in the balcony looking down at those men screaming at one another, you may wonder to which order *they* belong.

Remember, your leader may be a David.

"That's impossible!"

Is it? Most of us know at least two men in the lineage of David who have been damned and crucified by other men. By men who were absolutely certain the ones they were crucifying were *not* Davids.

And if you don't know of two such cases, for sure you know of one.

Men who go after the Sauls among us often crucify the Davids among us.

Who, then, can know who is a David and who is a Saul?

God knows. But he won't tell.

Are you so certain your king is a Saul and not a David that you are willing to take the position of God and go to war against your Saul? If so, then thank God you did not live in the days of crucifixion.

What, then, can you do? Very little. Perhaps nothing.

However, the passing of time (and the behavior of your leader while that time passes) reveals a great deal about your leader.

And the passing of time, and the way you react to that leader–be he David or Saul–reveals a great deal about *you.*

CHAPTER 17

TWO GENERATIONS after the reign of Saul, a young man enthusiastically enrolled himself into the ranks of Israel's army under a new king, the grandson of David. He soon began hearing tales of David's mighty men of valor. He set out to discover if one of those mighty men might still be alive and, if so, to find him and talk to him, though he calculated that such a man would be over a hundred years in age.

At last he discovered that, sure enough, one such man still lived. Having learned of his whereabouts, the youth hastened to his dwelling. Anxiously, if not hesitantly, he knocked on the door. Slowly it opened. There stood a giant of a man, gray . . . no, white haired . . . and wrinkled beyond expectation.

"Are you, sir, one of David's mighty men of long ago–one of those men of whom we have heard so much?"

For a long moment the old man surveyed the young man's face, his features, his uniform. Then, in an ancient but firm voice, he replied, never taking his steady gaze off the young man's face.

"If you are asking if I am a former thief and cave dweller and one who followed a sobbing, hysterical fugitive, then yes, I was one of the 'mighty men of David.'"

He straightened his shoulders with those last words. Nonetheless, his sentence ended in a chuckle.

"But, sir, you make the great king sound like a weakling. Was he not the greatest of all rulers?"

"He was no weakling," said the old man. Then sizing up the motivation for the eager young man's presence at his door, he replied wisely and softly, "Nor was he a great leader."

"Then what, good sir? For I have come to learn the ways of the great king and his . . . uh . . . mighty men. What *was* the greatness of David?"

"I see you have the ambitions typical of youth," said the old warrior. "I have the distinct notion you dream of leading men yourself one day." He paused, then continued reflectively. "Yes, I'll tell you of the greatness of my king, but my words may surprise you."

The old man's eyes filled with tears as he thought first of David and then of the foolish new king only recently crowned.

"I will tell you of my king and his greatness: My king never threatened me as yours does. Your new king has begun his reign with laws, rules, regulations, and fear. The clearest memory I have of my king, when we lived in the caves, is that his was a life of *submission.* Yes, David showed me submission, not authority. He taught me not the quick cure of rules and laws, but the art of patience. *That* is what changed my life. Legalism is nothing but a leader's way of avoiding suffering.

"Rules were invented by elders so they could get to bed early! Men who speak endlessly on authority only prove they have none. And kings who make speeches about submission only betray twin fears in their hearts: They are not certain they are really true leaders, sent of God. And they live in mortal fear of a rebellion.

"My king spoke not of submitting to him. He feared no rebellion . . . because he did not mind if he was dethroned!

"David taught me losing, not winning. Giving, not taking. He showed me that the leader, not the follower, is inconvenienced. David shielded us from suffering; he did not mete it out.

"He taught me that authority yields to rebellion, especially when that rebellion is nothing more dangerous than immaturity, or perhaps stupidity." The old man was obviously remembering some very tense and perhaps humorous episodes in the caves.

"No," he said, now in a voice with a touch of eloquence, "authority from God is not afraid of challengers, makes no defense, and cares not one whit if it must be dethroned.

"That was the greatness of the great . . . of the *true* king."

The old man began to walk away. Both anger and regal patience were evident in his bearing as he turned. Then he faced the youth once more, thundering one last salvo: "As far as David's having authority: Men who don't have it talk about it all the time. Submit, submit! That's all you hear. David had authority, but I don't think that fact ever occurred to him. We were six hundred no-goods with a leader who cried a lot. That's all we were!"

Those were the last words the young soldier heard from the old warrior. Slipping back into the street, he wondered if he would ever again be happy serving under Rehoboam.

CHAPTER 18

SO, HAVING COME TO THE END of our study of Saul and David, do you feel greatly assisted? What's that? You are now certain the man you are under is not truly from God . . . or if he is, he is at best only a Saul? My, how certain we mortals can be . . . of things even angels do not know.

May I ask you then, what you plan to do with this newly acquired knowledge? Yes, I am aware that you yourself are neither a Saul nor a David . . . but only a peasant of the realm. You do plan, though, to share your new discoveries with a few friends? I see. Then perhaps I should warn you that there is great danger with this heady new knowledge of yours. A strange mutation can take place within your own heart. You see, it is possible . . . but wait!

What is it I see over there? There . . . in that distant mist behind you. Turn. Do you see? Who is that figure making his way through the fog? It seems I have surely seen him before.

Look closely. Is it not possible for us to make out what he is doing?

He appears to be bending over some ancient chest. Yes, he has opened it.

Who is he? And what is he doing?

He has taken something out of the chest. A cloak? It is some kind of cape. Why, he is putting it on! The thing fits him perfectly, falling about his shoulders like a mantle.

Now what? He reaches again into that chest. I know I have seen that person somewhere before. What is it he pulls forth this time? A shield? No, a coat of arms. Yes, a coat of arms from some ancient, long-forgotten order. He holds it up as one who would make that order his own! Who is that man? The bearing. The stance. The carriage. I've seen it before. I'm sure.

Ah! He has moved out of the mist into the light. We will see him clearly now.

That face. Is it not you?!

Yes. It is. It is *you*! You who can so wisely discern the presence of an unworthy Saul!

Go! Look in yon mirror. That man is *you*! Look, too, at the name upon that coat of arms.

Behold: Absalom the Second!

PART 2

CHAPTER 19

"LOOK! HERE COMES DAVID!"

Bright smiles, a few giggles, some light laughter.

"See! It's David, no less."

Again, wide grins, a wave, and quiet amusement.

"That isn't King David," exclaimed a youth to his guardian as the two walked along the side of the street. "Why do they speak that way? That man is not David!"

"True, child, it is not David. It's only Absalom coming from the gate."

"Why do they call him David?" the boy asked, looking back over his shoulder at the handsome man in the chariot with the fifty men running before him.

"Because he reminds us all of David when he was young. And because we are all so glad that such a fine young man will take David's place someday. And perhaps, too, because Absalom is even better looking than David. He may be the most handsome man alive."

"Will Absalom be king soon? How old is King David, anyway? Is he about to die?"

"Of course not, my boy. Let's see . . . how old is David? Probably about the same age as King Saul when his reign came to an end."

"How old is Absalom?"

"About the same age as David when Saul was trying so hard to kill him."

"David is Saul's age. Absalom is the age of David when he first became king," mused the boy. They walked on silently for a while. The boy, obviously deep in thought, spoke again.

"Saul was very hard on David, was he not?"

"Yes, very."

"Is King David going to treat Absalom the same way Saul treated David? Will David be hard on Absalom?"

The guardian paused to consider the question, but the child went on: "If David treats Absalom badly, will Absalom behave with as much grace as David did?"

"Child, the future will surely tell us. My, you ask such questions! If, when you are grown, you can give answers as well as you now ask questions, you will surely be known as the wisest man on earth."

The two turned in at the palace gate.

CHAPTER 20

IT WARMED YOUR HEART TO KNOW a man who saw things so clearly. Discerning. Yes, that was the word that best described Absalom—*discerning*. He could penetrate to the heart of any problem.

Men felt secure just being with him. They even longed to have time with him. Talking with him, they realized that they themselves were wiser than they realized. Such a revelation made them feel good. As he discussed problem after problem and solution after solution, men began to long for the day when this one would be their leader. He could right so many wrongs. He gave them a sense of hope.

But this imposing, insightful man would never deliberately hasten the day of his own rule. They were confident of that. He was far too humble, too respectful of his father. And those around him began to feel a little frustrated that they would have to keep waiting for the better days of this man's rule.

The more they sat in his living room and talked, the more they realized that things were amiss in the kingdom. Yes, things amiss that they had never thought of before. And problems. Problems were coming to light of which they had never dreamed. Yes, they really were growing in wisdom and insight.

As the days passed, more and more of them came to listen. Word spread quietly. "Here is one who understands and has the answers." The frustrated came. They listened. They asked questions. They received excellent answers and began to hope.

Heads nodded. Dreams were born. As time passed, there were more such gatherings. Ideas turned into stories, stories of injustice that others might have deemed trivial. But not this listener! He was compassionate. And as those around him talked, the discovered injustices seemed to grow in number and severity. With each new story, men were more shocked at unfairness that was now, it seemed, rampant.

But the wise young man sat quietly and added not a word to these murmurings. He was too noble, you see. He always closed the evening conversations with a humble word of deference toward those in positions of responsibility. . . .

But it was too much to expect that any man could sit quietly by forever. This endless parade of injustice was bound to stir even the most respectful man. Even the purest in heart would be smitten with anger. (And this man was certainly the very purest in heart!)

Such a compassionate man could not forever turn his face from these sufferings nor forever remain silent. Such a noble character as this had to speak out someday.

Finally, his followers, which he vowed he did not have, were almost livid. Their insights into the wrongdoings of the kingdom not only grew but abounded. They all wanted to do something about these endless injustices.

At last, it seemed, the magnificent young man might concede. At the outset it was only a word. Later, a sentence. Men's hearts leaped. Joy, if not glee, reigned. Nobility was at last being aroused to action. But no! He cautioned them not to misunderstand. He was grieved, yes, but he could not speak against those in seats of responsibility. No, absolutely not. No matter how great the grievances, no matter how justified the frustration. He would not.

Yet he grieved more and more. It was obvious that some reports drove him to agony. Finally, his righteous anger broke out in cool, controlled words of strength. "These things ought not to be." He stood, eyes blazing. "If I were in responsibility, this is what I would do. . . ."

And with these words, the rebellion was ignited. Ignited in all but one, that is. In the man who seemed noblest and purest, this was not the case.

Rebellion had been in his heart for years.

CHAPTER 21

"SAGE!"

"Yes?"

"Sage, may I have a moment of your time?"

"Why, of course. I have a great deal of time."

"You have just come from a gathering of friends at Absalom's home?"

"Yes, that is correct."

"Would you mind sharing some of the impressions you had while there?"

"You mean a general impression of Absalom and his friends?"

"Yes, that would be good enough."

"Well, I have met many men like Absalom. Many."

"Then what is he like?"

"He is both sincere and ambitious. A contradiction, perhaps, but true, nonetheless. He probably means some of what he says. But his ambition will continue long after he discovers his inability to do the things he promises. Righting the wrongs always becomes secondary to ascent to power."

"I'm sorry, Sage, I do not understand."

"Two things stand out in my mind. At one gathering, when Absalom was answering questions, he was very emphatic that there should be more freedom in the kingdom. Everyone liked that. 'A people should be led only by God and not by men,' he said. 'Men should do only what they feel led of God to do. We should follow God, not a man.' I believe those were his words.

"At another meeting he spoke of the great visions he had for God's kingdom–of the great achievements the people were capable of. On the other hand, he spoke of many changes he would make in the way the kingdom is run. Although he did not seem to notice it, he had stated two irreconcilable propositions: many changes, more freedom.

"Yes, indeed, he does remind me of many other men I have encountered over the passing years."

"Sage, I think I understand what you've said, but I'm not sure what your point is."

"Absalom dreams. Dreams of what should be, of what *will* be: 'This is what *I* will do,' he says. But to fulfill those dreams, he must have the people's cooperation. Ah, this is the point often overlooked. Such dreams rest totally on the premise that the people of God will follow the new leader, that *all* will see as he sees. Such men as Absalom can envision no problems in their own future kingdom. Possibly the people *will* follow, but possibly they will not.

"At most, the Lord's people will follow a leader for a few years. They never support anyone very long. Generally, people do what they please. They can be stopped to do someone else's pleasure for a time, but not for long. People will not work too hard, even if they are following *God.*

"What will Absalom do when people stop following *him* willingly? Ah, now there is a question.

"You see, there is no kingdom without discord. Even God had his critics in heaven, you know. All kingdoms follow a bumpy course. And people, especially God's people, never follow any dream in unison. No, to accomplish all he spoke of tonight will take time. Not all will be willing to go along. Will he still be determined to put all his dreams into being? If so, then Absalom has but one recourse: *dictatorship*. Either that, or he will see few, if any, of his grand dreams accomplished. And if he does become a dictator, I can assure you that soon there will be discontent with *him*, just as there is now with the present king. Yes, if Absalom becomes king, soon thereafter you will see new meetings like the one we have just come from tonight . . . only with new faces, new dreams, and plans for a new rebellion. And that gathering will be against Absalom! Then, when *Absalom* hears of such a meeting and of discussion about a rebellion, he will have but one recourse."

"What do you feel he will do, Sage?"

"Rebels who ascend to the throne by rebellion have no patience with other rebels and their rebellions. When Absalom is faced with rebellion, he will become a tyrant. He will bring ten times the evil he sees in your present king. He will squelch rebellion and rule with an iron hand . . . and by fear. He will eliminate all opposition. This is always the final stage of high-sounding rebellions. Such will be Absalom's way if he takes the throne from David."

"But, Sage, have not some rebellions been of benefit, throwing out brutes and despots?"

"Oh, yes, a few. But I remind you: This particular kingdom is different from all others. This kingdom is composed of God's people. It is a spiritual kingdom. I tell you emphatically, no rebellion in the kingdom of God is proper, nor can it ever be fully blessed."

"Why do you say this, Sage?"

"For many reasons. One is obvious. In the spiritual realm, those who lead rebellions have already proven, no matter how grandiose their words or angelic their ways, that they have a critical nature, an unprincipled character, and hidden motives in their hearts. Frankly, they are thieves. They create dissatisfaction and tension within the realm and then either seize power or siphon off followers. They use their followers to found their own dominions. Such a sorry beginning, built on the foundation of insurrection. . . . No, God never honors division in his realm.

"I find it curious that those who feel qualified to split God's kingdom do not feel capable of going somewhere else–to another land–to raise up a completely new kingdom. No, they must steal from another leader. I have never seen the exception. They seem always to need at least a few prepackaged followers.

"Beginning empty-handed and alone frightens the best of men. It also speaks volumes of just how sure they are that God is with them. Their every word, if truly understood, tells of their insecurity.

"There are many lands unspoiled and unpossessed. There are many people in other places waiting to follow a true king, a true man of God. Why don't 'would-be kings and prophets' simply walk quietly away, alone, then find another people in another place, and there raise up the kingdom they envision?

"Those who lead rebellions in the spiritual world are unworthy. There are no exceptions. And now I must go. I must join the passing parade."

"Tell me, Sage, what is your name?"

"My name? I am History."

CHAPTER 22

DAVID STOOD ON THE BALCONY overlooking the gardened terrace of his palace. The lights from the houses in the Holy City twinkled below him. From behind, a man approached. David sighed and, without turning, spoke. "Yes, Joab, what is it?"

"Have you heard?"

"Yes, I've heard," he replied quietly.

"How long have you known?" asked Joab with anxious surprise.

"For months, years, perhaps a decade. Perhaps I have known for thirty years."

Joab was not sure, after this answer, if they were speaking of the same subject. Absalom, after all, was not much past thirty. "Sir, I speak of Absalom," he said a little hesitantly.

"As do I," said the king.

"If you have known so long, why did you not stop him?"

"I was just asking myself that same question."

"Shall I stop him for you?"

David whirled round! In one instant, Joab's query had resolved his dilemma.

"No! Nor shall you speak one word to him. Nor shall you criticize him. Nor shall you allow anyone else to speak critically of him or what he is doing. Certainly you shall not stop him."

"But will he not then take the kingdom?"

David sighed again, softly, slowly. For a moment he balanced between tears and a smile. Then he smiled lightly and said, "Yes, perhaps he will."

"What will you do? Do you have plans?"

"No. None. Quite frankly, I have no idea what to do. I have fought many battles and faced many sieges. I have usually known what to do. But for this occasion, I have only the experience of my youth to draw on. The course I followed at that time seems to be the best I can follow now."

"And what course was that?"

"To do absolutely nothing."

CHAPTER 23

DAVID WAS ALONE AGAIN. Slowly, quietly, he walked the length of his rooftop garden. Finally he paused and spoke aloud to himself.

"I have waited, Absalom. I have waited and watched for years. I have asked again and again, 'What is in the heart of this young man?' And now I know. You will do the unthinkable. You will divide the very kingdom of God. All else was talk."

David was quiet for a moment. Then, almost in awe, he spoke, his voice hushed. "Absalom does not hesitate to divide the *kingdom of God.*

"Now I know. He seeks followers. Or at least he does not turn them away. Though he seems magnificently pure and noble, still he divides. His followers grow, even though he states convincingly that he has none."

For a long time David said nothing. Finally, with a trace of humor in his words, he began to address himself. "All right, good King David, you have one issue resolved. You are in the middle of a division, and you may very well be dethroned. Now, to the second issue." He paused, lifted his hand and, almost fatally, asked, "What will you *do*?

"The kingdom hangs in the balance. It seems I have two choices: to lose everything or to be a Saul. I can stop Absalom. I need only to be a Saul. In my old age, shall I now become a Saul? I feel the Lord himself awaits my decision.

"Shall I now be a Saul?" he asked himself again, this time loudly.

A voice from behind answered, "Good King, he has been no David to you."

David turned. It was Abishai who had approached unannounced.

"A crowded place, this terrace," quipped David.

"Sir?" said Abishai.

"Nothing. Suffice it to say I have not been without visitors today–a day when I would have chosen solitude. What did you say to me? In fact, what did I say?"

"You said, 'Shall I be a Saul to Absalom?' and I replied, 'He has been no young David to you.'"

"I never challenged Saul; I never attempted to divide the kingdom during his reign. Is that what you are saying?"

"More," replied Abishai strongly. "Saul was evil toward you and made your life torture. You responded only with respect and private agony. The bad things that happened in those days came only from one side. All fell on you. Yet you could have divided the kingdom and probably could have overthrown Saul. But rather than do that, you left the kingdom. You fled rather than cause division. You risked your life for unity and sealed your lips and eyes to all his injustices. You had more cause to rebel than any man in the history of this–or of any kingdom that has ever been. Absalom has to twist hard to conjure up his list of injustices . . . few of them significant, I might add.

"Has Absalom behaved as you did? Has Absalom respected you? Does Absalom seek to preserve the kingdom? Does he refuse to speak against you? Does Absalom turn aside followers? Has

Absalom left the land to prevent its being sundered? Is Absalom respectful? Does he bear suffering in silent agony? Have bad things fallen on Absalom?

"No, he is only pure and noble!"

Abishai's last words came out almost in bites. Then he continued, more gravely this time.

"His grievances are minor compared to your rightful grievances toward Saul. You never mistreated Saul. And you have never, in any way, been unfair to Absalom."

David interrupted with a grin. "I seem to have a gift for making old men and young men hate me without a cause. In my youth, the old attacked me; when I am old, the young attack me. What a marvelous achievement."

"My point," continued Abishai, "is that Absalom is no David. Therefore I ask you: Why don't you stop his rebellion? Stop him, the miserable . . ."

"Careful, Abishai. Remember he is also a son of the king. We should never speak ill of the son of a king."

"Good King, I remind you that you refused to raise your sword or your spear even once against Saul. But Absalom speaks against you night and day. He will one day–soon–raise an army against you. Nay, a nation. *This* nation! Young Absalom is no young David. I counsel you to stop him!"

"You are asking me, Abishai, to become a Saul," David replied heavily.

"No, I'm simply saying he is no David. Stop him!"

"And if I stop him, will I still be a David? If I stop him, will I not be a Saul?" asked the king, his eyes piercing Abishai. "To stop him, I must become either a Saul or an Absalom."

"My king and my friend, I speak to you fondly: I sometimes think you are a bit insane."

"Yes, I can see why," chuckled David.

"Dear King, Saul was a bad king. Absalom is, in some ways, a youthful incarnation of Saul. You alone are constant. You are forever the brokenhearted shepherd boy. Tell me truthfully, what do you plan?"

"Until now, I have not been sure. But of this I am certain: In my youth I was no Absalom. And in my old age I shall not be a Saul. In my youth, by your own words, I was David. In my old age I intend to be David still. Even if it costs me a throne, a kingdom, and perhaps my head."

Abishai said nothing for a while. Then, slowly, he spoke, making sure he grasped the significance of David's decision.

"You were not an Absalom, and you refuse to be a Saul. Sir, if you are not willing to put Absalom down, then I suggest we prepare to evacuate the kingdom. For Absalom will surely take the throne."

"Only as surely as King Saul killed the shepherd boy," replied the wise old king.

"What?" asked Abishai, startled.

"Think on it, Abishai. God once delivered a defenseless shepherd boy from the powerful, mad king. He can yet deliver an old ruler from an ambitious young rebel."

"You underestimate your adversary," retorted Abishai.

"You underestimate my God," replied David serenely.

"But why, David? Why not fight?"

"I will give you the answer. And you will recall–for you were there–that I once gave this same answer to Joab in a cave long ago!

"It is better that I be defeated, even killed, than to learn the ways of . . . of a Saul or the ways of an Absalom. The kingdom is not that valuable. Let him have it, if that be the Lord's will. I repeat: I *shall not* learn the ways of either Saul or Absalom.

"And now, being an old man, I will add a word I might not have known then. Abishai, no man knows his own heart. I certainly do not know mine. Only God does. Shall I defend my little realm in the name of God? Shall I throw spears, and plot and divide . . . and kill men's spirits if not their bodies . . . to protect *my* empire? I did not lift a finger to be *made* king. Nor shall I do so to preserve a kingdom. Even the kingdom of God! God put me here. It is not my responsibility to take, or *keep*, authority. Do you not realize, it may be *his* will for these things to take place? If he chooses, God can protect and keep the kingdom even now. After all, it is *his* kingdom.

"As I said, no man knows his own heart. I do not know mine. Who knows what is really in my heart? Perhaps in God's eyes I am no longer worthy to rule. Perhaps he *is* through with me. Perhaps it is his will for Absalom to rule. I honestly don't know. And if this is his will, I want it. God may be finished with me!

"Any young rebel who raises his hand against a Saul, or any old king who raises his hand against an Absalom, may–in truth–be raising his hand against the will of God.

"In either case, I shall raise no hand! Wouldn't I look a little strange trying to stay in control if God desires that I fall?"

"But you know that Absalom should not be king!" replied Abishai in frustration.

"Do I? No man knows. Only God knows, and he has not spoken. I did not fight to be king, and I will not fight to remain king. May God come tonight and take the throne, the kingship, and . . ." David's voice faltered. "And his *anointing* from me. I seek his will, not his power. I repeat, I desire his will more than I desire a position of leadership. He may be through with me."

"King David?" A voice came from behind the two men.

"Yes? Oh, a messenger. What is it?"

"Absalom. He wishes to see you a moment. He wants to ask permission to go to Hebron to make a sacrifice."

"David," said Abishai hoarsely, "you know what that really means, don't you?"

"Yes, I do."

David turned to the messenger. "Tell Absalom I will be there in a moment."

David looked one last time at the quiet city below, then turned and walked toward the door.

"*Will* you let him go to Hebron?" Abishai demanded.

"I will," said the great king. "Yes, I will."

Then he turned to the messenger. "This is a dark hour for me. When I have finished speaking to Absalom, I shall retire. Tomorrow have one of the prophets come to me for consultation. Or a scribe. On second thought, send me Zadok, the high priest. Ask him to join me here after the evening sacrifice."

Abishai called out once more, softly this time. Admiration flashed across his face. "Good King, thank you."

"For what?" the puzzled king asked as he turned back in the doorway.

"Not for what you have done, but for what you have *not* done. Thank you for not throwing spears, for not rebelling against kings, for not exposing a man in authority when he was so very vulnerable, for not dividing a kingdom, for not attacking young Absaloms who look like young Davids but are not."

He paused. "And thank you for suffering, for being willing to lose everything. Thank you for giving God a free hand to end, and even destroy, your kingdom–if it pleases him. Thank you for being an example to us all.

"And most of all," he chuckled, "thank you for not consulting witches."

CHAPTER 24

"NATHAN!"

"Yes? Oh, it's you, Zadok."

"You will pardon my intrusion, Nathan, but I have been observing you for several moments now. You were about to enter the throne room, I believe, to see King David?"

"Yes, Zadok. That was my intent, but I have thought better of it. The king has no need of me."

"I am disappointed, Nathan. In my judgment the king has great need of you. He is facing the gravest test of his life. I am not sure he can pass a test as demanding as this one."

"He has *already* passed this test, Zadok," countered Nathan with a sureness in his voice that showed him to be a prophet of God.

"David has already passed this test? Forgive me, Nathan, but I have no idea what you mean. This crisis, as you well know, has just begun."

"Zadok, your king passed *this* test long ago, when he was a young man."

"You speak of Saul? But that, my friend, was a wholly different matter."

"Not at all. It is *exactly* the same. There is really no difference at all. As David related to his God and to the man over him at that time long ago . . . so now David will also relate to his God and to the man under him. There can be no difference. Not ever.

"True, circumstances may be altered . . . slightly. Ever so slightly, I might add. But the heart! Ah, the heart is always the same.

"Zadok, I have always been grateful Saul was our *first* king. I shudder to think of the trouble he might have caused if, as a young man, he had found himself under some other king. There is no real difference between the man who discovers a Saul in his life and the man who finds an Absalom in his life. In either situation, the corrupt heart will find its 'justification.' The Sauls of this world can never see a David; they see only Absalom. The Absaloms of this world can never see a David; they see only Saul."

"And the pure heart?" asked Zadok.

"Ah, now there is a rare thing indeed. How does a man with a broken heart handle an Absalom? The way he handled a Saul? We will soon know, Zadok!"

"You and I were not privileged to be there when David came to his hour with Saul. But we are privileged to be present in his hour with Absalom. I for one intend to watch this unfolding drama very closely. And in so doing, I have the good expectation of learning a lesson or two. Mark my words, David will work his way through this thing–and he will pass this test with the same grace he displayed in his youth."

"And Absalom?"

"What of Absalom?"

"In a few hours he may be our king. Is that not your point?"

"There is that possibility," replied Zadok, almost with humor.

Nathan laughed. "If Absalom gains the throne, may heaven have mercy on all the Sauls, Davids, *and* Absaloms of the realm!

"In my judgment our young Absalom will make a splendid Saul," continued Nathan as he turned and strolled down the long corridor.

"Yes. A splendid Saul. For in every way but age and position, Absalom is already a Saul."

CHAPTER 25

"I THANK YOU FOR COMING, ZADOK."

"My king."

"You are a priest of God. Could you tell me a story of long ago?"

"What story, my king?"

"Do you know the story of Moses?"

"I do."

"Tell it to me."

"It is long; shall I tell it all?"

"No, not all."

"Then what part?"

"Tell me about Korah's rebellion."

The high priest stared at David with eyes burning. David stared back, his also ablaze. The two men understood.

"I shall tell you the story of Korah's rebellion and of Moses' behavior in the midst of that rebellion.

"Many have heard the story of Moses. He is the supreme

example of the Lord's anointed. God's true government rests upon a man–no, upon the contrite heart of a man. There is no form or order to God's government; there is only a man or woman with a contrite heart. Moses was such a man.

"Korah was not such a man, although he was the first cousin of Moses. Korah wanted the authority Moses had. One peaceful morning, Korah awoke. There was no discord among God's people that morning, but before the day was over he had found 252 men to agree with his charges against Moses."

"Then there were problems in the nation when Moses ruled?" asked David.

"There are always problems in any kingdom," replied Zadok. "Always. Furthermore, the ability to be able to see those problems is a cheap gift, indeed."

David smiled and asked, "But, Zadok, you know there have been unjust kingdoms and unjust rulers and pretenders and liars who have ruled and governed. How can a simple people know which is a kingdom with faults but led by men of God, and which is a kingdom unworthy of men's submission? How can a people know?"

David stopped; he realized that he had hit upon what he wished most of all to know. Heavily, he spoke again. "And the king–how can he know? Can he know if he is just? Can he know if the charges are of great worth? Are there signs?" David's final words were anxious.

"Are you looking for some list let down from heaven, David? Even if there were such a list, even if there were a way to know, wicked men would arrange their kingdoms to fit the list! And if such a list existed and a good man filled it to perfection, there would be rebels claiming he had not fulfilled one qualification listed therein. You underestimate the human heart, David."

"Then how shall the people know?"

"They cannot know."

"You mean that in the midst of a hundred voices making a thousand claims, the simple people of God have no assurance of who is truly anointed to bear God's authority and who is not?"

"They can never be certain."

"Who, then, can know?"

"God always knows–but he does not tell."

"Is there no hope, then, for those who must follow unworthy men?"

"Their grandchildren will be able to see the matter clearly. *They* will know. But those caught up in the drama? They can never be certain. Nonetheless, a good thing will come from it all."

"What is that?"

"As surely as the sun rises, people's hearts will be tested. Despite the many claims–and counterclaims–the hidden motives within the hearts of all who are involved will be revealed. This might not seem important in the eyes of men, but in the eyes of God such things are central. The motives of the heart will eventually be revealed. God will see to it."

"I despise such tests," replied David wearily. "I hate such nights as this one. Yet God seems to send many, many things into my life to test this heart of mine. Once more, this night, I find my heart on trial.

"Zadok, there is something that bothers me above all else. Perhaps God *is* finished with me. Is there not some way for me to know?"

"I know of no other ruler in all history who would even ask the question, Good King. Most other men would have ripped their opponent–or even their imagined opponent–to shreds by now. But to answer your questions, I know of no way for you to be certain that God is–or is not–finished with you."

David sighed and choked back a sob. "Then continue with the story. Korah had 252 followers, did he? What happened next?"

"Korah approached Moses and Aaron with his followers. He informed Moses that he had no right to all the authority he exercised."

"Well, we Hebrews are consistent, aren't we?" laughed David.

"No, the heart of man is consistent, David," replied Zadok.

"Tell me, what was Moses' response to Korah?"

"At the age of forty, Moses had been an arrogant, self-willed man, not unlike Korah. What he might have done at forty, I cannot say. At eighty, he was a broken man. He was . . ."

"The meekest man who ever lived," interrupted David.

"The man who carries the rod of God's authority should be. Otherwise God's people will live in terror. Yes, a broken man faced Korah. And I believe you already know what Moses did, David. He did . . . nothing."

"Nothing. Ah, what a man."

"He fell on his face before God. That is all he did."

"Why did he do that, Zadok?"

"David, you of all men must know. Moses knew that God alone had put him in charge of Israel. There was nothing that needed to be done. Korah and his 252 followers would seize the kingdom–or God would vindicate Moses. Moses knew that."

"Men would find it hard to imitate such a life, would they not? An imposter surely could not fake such surrender, could he? But tell me, how did God vindicate Moses?"

"Moses told the men to return the next day with censers and incense . . . and God would decide the issue."

"So!" cried David. "So!" he exclaimed again even louder. "Sometimes God *does* tell," he said excitedly. "Please continue."

"Korah and two of his friends were swallowed by the earth. The other 250 died by . . ."

"Never mind," said David. "Suffice it to say that Moses was proven to be in authority . . . by God! God *did* tell! The people knew who really had authority from God, and at last Moses had rest."

"No, David. He did not find rest, and the people were not satisfied with God's answer! The very next day the whole congregation murmured against Moses, and they would all have died except for the prayers of Moses."

"And men fight to become kings!" David shook his head in perplexity.

Zadok paused, then continued: "David, I perceive that you are torn by the question of what is true authority and what is not. You want to know what to do with a rebellion, if indeed it is a rebellion and not the hand of God. I trust you will find the only pure thing to do–and do it. And thereby you will teach us all."

The door opened, and Abishai rushed in. "Good King! Your son, your own flesh and blood, has proclaimed himself *king* in Hebron. At first impression, it seems all Israel has gone over to him. He plans to take the throne. He marches toward Jerusalem. Some of the men closest to you have gone over to him."

David walked away. He spoke quietly to himself. "Israel's third king? Do true leaders of the kingdom of God gain authority in this way?"

Zadok, not certain if he should be hearing David's words or not, spoke out. "My king?"

David turned, his eyes moist.

"At last," David said quietly. "At last this matter will be resolved. Perhaps tomorrow someone besides God will know."

"Perhaps," said Zadok, "but perhaps not. Such questions may be debated even after we are all dead."

"That might also be tomorrow," laughed David. "Go, Abishai, tell Joab. You will find him in the turret of the east wall."

Abishai departed as he had entered, in haste and in fury.

"I wonder, Zadok," mused David, "if a man can force God into a position where he *must* tell."

CHAPTER 26

ABISHAI RUSHED ACROSS THE COURTYARD and into the eastern rampart, where he charged up the spiral staircase. At the top of the stairs, Joab stared down at Abishai. In the flickering light of torches, each man studied the face of the other.

Abishai spoke. "Have you heard, Joab?"

"Have I heard! 'Tis midnight, yet half the city is awake with the word. How can it be, Abishai–a son against his own father!"

"When kingdoms are vulnerable, men see queer sights," responded Abishai with a distant stare.

"And they'll sacrifice anything to satisfy ambition," added Joab angrily. "What think you of these things, Abishai?"

"What think I?" responded Abishai, matching Joab's anger with his own rage. "This! Absalom has no authority in the kingdom. He holds no power, no office, yet he has risen up to divide the kingdom. He has raised his hand against the very anointed of

God–against David! David–who has never done or spoken one evil word against him.

"What think I?" Abishai's voice rose toward a crescendo. "If Absalom, who has no authority, will commit this deed; if Absalom, who is nothing, will divide the very kingdom of God–" His voice now rolled like thunder. "If Absalom will do these evil things *now*, what in the name of sanity might that man do if he be *king*?"

CHAPTER 27

DAVID AND ZADOK WERE ALONE ONCE MORE.

"And now, what will you do, David? In your youth, you spoke no word against an unworthy king. What will you do now with an equally unworthy youth?"

"As I said," replied David, "these are the times I hate the most, Zadok. Nonetheless, against all reason, I judge my own heart first and rule against its interests. I will do what I did under Saul. I will leave the destiny of the kingdom in God's hands alone. Perhaps he is finished with me. Perhaps I have sinned too greatly and am no longer worthy to lead. Only God knows if that is true, and it seems he will not tell."

Then, clenching his fist, yet with a touch of wry humor in his voice, David added emphatically, "But today I shall give ample space for this untelling God of ours to show us his will. I know of no other way to bring about such an extraordinary event except by doing *nothing*! The throne is not mine. Not to have, not to take, not to protect, and not to keep.

"I will leave the city. The throne is the Lord's. So is the kingdom. I will not hinder God. No obstacle, no activity on my part lies between me and God's will. Nothing will prevent him from accomplishing his will. If I am not to be king, God will find no difficulty in making Absalom to be Israel's king. Now it is possible. God shall be God!"

The true king turned and walked quietly out of the throne room, out of the palace, out of the city. He walked and he walked . . .

Into the bosoms of all men whose hearts are pure.

Well, dear reader, the time has come for us to say good-bye once more. I will leave you to your thoughts and to reflect on the hidden motives of your own heart.

Oh, by the way, the players are working on a love story. Perhaps we can see it together when it is performed. I believe it shall be called . . . The Divine Romance.

I trust, then, by the mercy of God, we shall meet again.

Book Discussion Guide

1. How can you break the cycle of wounding? What makes this hard to accomplish?
2. God's prophet had anointed David when he was a boy, but for years David saw only hardship and danger. How can a person remain faithful between the promise and the payoff? What might make it difficult to remain faithful even after the payoff has arrived?
3. Have you been broken? Why do we tend to avoid this? Is it always necessary? Are you willing to live through pain, or do you avoid it? When do you most clearly see the sufficiency of God's grace?
4. Who throws spears at you? How does God want you to respond?
5. Are you clinging to God's promises or to God himself? What is the distinction (if any)?
6. Chapter 6 deals largely with God's divine establishment of authority. Read Romans 13 and consider your reaction to these concepts. What do you find hard to swallow? Are there any exceptions to this general rule?

7. Do you agree with the author's assertion that God knows, but he never tells us? How does your answer affect your view of God's relationship with his children?
8. What needs to happen to put your own inner Saul to death?
9. David's men saw the opportunity as a sign from God, but David refused to harm Saul. If an opportunity arose, would you do something drastic to ensure your own safety? to exact justice? to take revenge?
10. The author points out that God does not rescind his gifts, even when people use them unfaithfully. (But contrast the story of Samson in Judges 16.) What does this show about God's character?
11. Do you know any Davids who have been condemned as Sauls?
12. What makes a true leader? How should a real leader approach and handle his or her authority?
13. The author equates rebellion with thievery, taking what is not rightfully one's own. Do you agree with the author's statement that "no rebellion in the Kingdom of God is proper" (page 71)? What differentiates dissenters or reformers from schismatics and dividers? How would you apply these truths to historical events like the Protestant Reformation or the American Revolution?
14. Do you agree with David's commitment to "raise no hand," or do you find this course too passive? How can we know when God wants us to take action and when he wants us to accept action taken against us?
15. In this story, David considered the throne to be God's, not his own to have, to take, to protect, to keep. He asserted that he desired God's will more than God's blessing (see page 79).

Could you say the same about what God has given you? How would you respond if your job, your home, your family were all taken from you?

16. Sauls see only Absaloms; Absaloms see only Sauls. Neither can recognize a David. How can we distinguish one from the others? Is it true that we can never be certain whether a leader is a Saul or a David, that only God can truly know?
17. The person who wields the rod of God's authority should be the meekest, a broken man, lest his people live in terror. What kind of authority does a true leader have? How should he or she respond to that commission? How should his or her followers respond to that individual?

THE PRISONER IN THE THIRD CELL

To my youngest and much loved daughter, Cindy

* * *

It has been said that it is impossible to forgive a man who deliberately hurts you for the sole purpose of destroying you or lowering you. If this be true, you have but one hope: to see this unfair hurt as coming by permission from God for the purpose of lifting your stature above that place where formerly you stood.

Prologue

"THE NEW PRISONER HAS ARRIVED, CAPTAIN."

"Is the rumor true?" the captain responded.

Without answering, the guard held up a piece of papyrus for Protheus to see.

"Herod has lost his mind. He will yet be found as mad as his father.

"Making *this* man a prisoner," he continued, "may very well set off a revolution. The common people are enraged."

"Sir, forgive me, but I must speak. I do not like this," said one of the guards in a voice shaking with emotion. "I do not want him here. I do not want his blood on my hands. I fear that man. I listened to him once, in the desert. I fear what God might do to us for imprisoning such a man."

"Do your duty, soldier. Prepare a cell."

"Only one is empty, sir."

"Prepare it then."

"There is nothing to prepare, sir. It is the *third* cell."

"The pit? We shall see a holy man of God vanquished to *that*?"

"Sir, there is something about all this I dislike more than anything else."

"What is that, soldier?"

"I dread what we are going to have to listen to from the other two prisoners when they find out who is in cell three."

"I cannot say I disagree with you," sighed Protheus.

At that moment the door at the head of the stairs swung open. In the doorway could be seen the silhouette of two soldiers and a prisoner.

"I wonder how long Herod will let him live," thought the captain to himself.

He who takes up the sword perishes by the sword.
He who refuses to take up the sword perishes on the cross.

CHAPTER 1

ELIZABETH OPENED THE DOOR to her home, there to be greeted by a young kinsman from Bethlehem.

"I have an urgent message for you from Joseph and Mary."

"Come in," responded Elizabeth. At that moment Zachariah entered the room carrying a young three-year-old boy in his arms.

"I have a message and a small package, both from Joseph and Mary."

"Please," said Elizabeth. "My eyes have long since lost their ability to read such small letters."

The young man broke the wax seal of the small scroll, cleared his throat, and began.

> *"Strange things have taken place in our lives of late, events as unusual as those that brought forth the birth of your son and ours. We had a visit from three Babylonian astrologers just yesterday. Then, last night, Joseph had a dream, a very disturbing dream. In it, our son was seen in grave danger from the wrath of that monster, Herod*

the Great. We are departing Bethlehem at this very hour. Joseph and I are going to Egypt, there to remain until this dreadful danger, whatever it is, passes.

"But our son is not the only one in danger. We fear that John is, also. Perhaps all the young firstborn children in Judea are in danger. Elizabeth, we urge you and Zachariah to leave Judea immediately. Go where you wish, but your nearest, safest hiding place is the desert. With this letter we are sending a small package. If I do not explain, you will wonder forever what a poor carpenter and his wife are doing owning gold. The Babylonian astrologers gave several gifts to us. One of them was a casket of gold coins. We are sharing them with the three of you. Please, in the name of our God, flee Judea today. Tomorrow may be too late. We will try to find you on some better day when, hopefully, we return from Egypt."

The letter was signed by Joseph and Mary.

With that, the young man handed a small leather pouch to Zachariah, which he quickly opened. Inside the pouch were several gold coins. For a moment no one spoke.

Elizabeth, ignoring the gift, broke the silence. "I am not surprised about Herod. The enemy of God would do just such a thing. We must leave immediately."

Zachariah now addressed the young courier.

"Go. And tell no one of this." With those simple words, the youth bowed his head in respect and departed.

"You are right, Elizabeth. We must leave for the desert immediately."

"How can we survive out there? In order to be completely safe, we must go far into the desert. Can anyone *survive* out there?"

"Elizabeth, it will be a difficult thing for all of us, to say the least. But the Essenes survive out there. They have families; they have children; they have homes out there. Our son *will* survive." Zachariah then chuckled, "Perhaps you and I may even survive there, at least for a little while."

CHAPTER 2

THE WINDS WERE DEADLY. The heat was more than Zachariah or Elizabeth ever imagined. Canyon walls were like a furnace. Even the blowing sand scalded the face, trying, it seemed, to destroy anything that dared walk into that living furnace. Water was scarce, food nonexistent. In the midst of murderous heat, Zachariah had fainted on several occasions.

Finally, after a week's journey into that boiling hell, the three wayfarers arrived at one of the Essene villages. After several days of rest, they penetrated even deeper into this oven of sand and rock. At last they came to the largest of the Essene settlements.

The three were received with gracious reserve by the sober-faced Essenes. Within a few weeks the elderly couple and their young son had become a part of this strange community of religious stoics.

Zachariah became ill almost immediately. Nowhere in this inferno could he find a hiding place from the all-pervasive temperatures. The old man knew his death was but a matter of days.

His last hours were spent being cared for by women of the village who mercifully wrapped his body in wet rags. Finally, late into the night when heat was at its lowest, Zachariah gave his life up to God, leaving a widow and a small child.

During the ensuing years, young John took his place among the Essenes, eventually becoming one of them. From the beginning, the lad seemed to have a natural disposition for the communal life of this desert hermitage.

The wilderness heat eventually took its toll on Elizabeth, for the elderly did not live long in this scorched world. Even as Elizabeth's strength was waning and her steps grew fewer, word came that Herod was dead. Immediately she made plans to return to her home in the cool hills of Judea. With her last good strength, and the aid of several Essenes, she and her son returned safely to her Judean home. But not long after John's twelfth birthday, Elizabeth joined Zachariah in death. John was now an orphan. Elizabeth's closet kinsmen buried her not far from that very place where an angel once visited her and told her that she would bear one of the most incredible children ever to make entrance into this world.

Where would John live now that his parents were both dead? Who would raise this boy to manhood? These were the questions that filled everyone's mind as John and his kinsmen returned to his house.

CHAPTER 3

"JOHN, WE GRIEVE FOR THE PASSING of your mother." The voice was that of Hannel, one of Israel's most devout laymen. "Nonetheless, a decision is in order. Tomorrow each of us must return to our separate homes. It is for you to decide which one of us you will live with. Though I am not one of your close kin, I have come here because I know of your devotion to the Hebrew religion, and I have spoken often with your mother about adopting you if the providence of God ever brought forth such a need.

"John, I am very aware of how you feel about your future, that you must one day serve God. In my judgment, the best possible course for you is to come live with me. God has been very good to me, John. Ours is a very devout home. There is prayer; there is fasting. My entire family is devoted to God. I even own several scrolls of holy writ. Few homes are so honored.

"I pledge to you now, in the sight of your relatives, that you will be trained by the best of the rabbis. I commit to you the promise of the best religious education possible. We have a large home. It is quite comfortable. You may spend as much time in prayer as you wish. You may come and go in pursuit of your religious training as you please. When you reach the age of twenty-one, if you desire, you may go to the temple in Jerusalem and study under the Pharisees or be trained to become a temple priest. Though you are of the tribe of Judah and not a Levi, you would be allowed into any of the religious orders, including the Levitical priesthood, because you have taken the vow of the Nazarite."

Hannel paused. John said nothing, nor did he betray any of his feelings.

It was Parnach, a cousin of Zachariah and a man of influence, power, and wealth, who spoke next.

"John, it is true that you may wish to continue to pursue your Nazarite vow. On the other hand, the day may come when you might decide to take some other direction in your life. If you would come to live with me, I will promise you the best education in Israel. I need not tell you of my place in government. I am in the highest echelon of power. You will grow up among the most influential men in our country, for my friends include even its greatest rulers. I have position, prestige, and access to power. Whatever your goal in life, as a member of my house you will be friends of those men who have the greatest influence to help you bring about your goals. I would strongly urge you to come and be part of my household."

Once more John said nothing.

Now it was Joseph and Mary's turn. Mary spoke.

"John, we have very little to offer you. Mostly, the companionship of your cousins. We have a large family. You and my oldest son have always enjoyed one another's company. But if you would come with us, you would work in a carpenter's shop. I suppose in the light of what these men have offered you, it would be wise for you to go with one of them. I am almost embarrassed to invite you to our home. As I said, we are poor, but you will be loved."

"I know," responded John finally. "If I must choose between Hannel, Parnach, and your family, then I would choose the latter."

"Then you will come and live with us?"

"No," replied John, looking calmly into the face of Mary.

Mary inadvertently slipped her hand to her mouth. "It's the Essenes, is it not?" Mary paused, and her face signaled that she desired a clear response.

"Yes, it is. I belong there."

A moment of silence ensued.

"John," continued Mary, "perhaps you do not know this, but several Essene families have moved to Nazareth. Do you remember the two little boys you used to play with there . . . and oh, yes . . . and that little green-eyed . . ."

"Mary," interrupted John, speaking strongly, almost sternly, and very much out of character for a Hebrew lad. "I know what I am to do. The Lord has made this very clear to me. I am to return to the desert, and I am to live there." John now turned toward Hannel and Parnach.

"I wish to thank both of you for your kind offers. You have all been gracious and caring. Thank you for your concern for my future. Nonetheless, I know where I belong. I am returning to the desert."

Once more John turned to face Mary.

"You are my mother's closest friend. She loved you dearly. She spoke often of you. Nonetheless, I must leave here immediately, *alone.* The Lord has taken my father and my mother. I have absolutely no obligations. I have no brothers or sisters, no grandparents." John paused. "You must not worry about me; and though it may seem to all of you that I have simply disappeared, I will be well. God *will* take care of me.

"I am not sure of much, except that I *must* live in the wilderness until God tells me otherwise. This I also know: Out among the Essenes I will discover what it is that my God wishes me to do. The desert will provide me with the answers. My preparation for His will is not in a city nor a village, but a desert."

The next morning a boy not yet thirteen bade good-bye to Parnach and Hannel, to Joseph and Mary, and to his second cousin who was a year younger than he, who bore the name Jesus.

CHAPTER 4

JOHN TOOK HIS PLACE ONCE AGAIN among the Essenes, but allowed no one to adopt him. He lived alone. To provide his meager needs for food, water, and clothing, he worked with his hands.

Never once in the coming years did John touch wine. His hair grew, uncut, from the day of his birth. But because it was the one possible source of pride in his life, he gave even his long raven hair the minimum of attention, obscuring its length and beauty.

Much of this time John spent in prayer and fasting–so often so that his fingers sometimes turned purple, and he was sometimes so weak that his legs could no longer support his frame. Frequently he spent whole days and nights in unbroken prayer, doing little to protect his body from the harsh elements of the wilderness. Austere was the way he lived; stern became his demeanor.

As the years passed on, John began spending his time wandering the desert. There the fierce sun leathered his face and turned it to craggy wrinkles. By the time he reached manhood, the son of Zachariah and Elizabeth looked far, far older than his age. To John, such things were a small price to pay, for his long treks into the desert were his most coveted times. There he could spend uninterrupted hours alone with God. The howling wind, the furnace heat, the baking sun, and the cutting sand became his closest companions.

As he approached the age of thirty, when, by tradition, holy men might end their training and enter the ministry, John was one who could hear the voice of God within the desert wind, see His face within the sun, and feel His presence in the blowing sand. He was by now both a mystery and a legend among the Essenes. Few men, the Essenes were certain, had ever lived their lives so completely before God. Few men had abandoned every human comfort to be so utterly unhindered in their pursuit of knowing the Lord. In the minds of the Essenes, and even among some of the nomadic tribes, there was no doubt that a prophet was being raised up in their midst. The desert was giving birth to a man of God.

Such a man as John the world had rarely seen. His devotion to God was absolute; his life was void of all except his call to speak for God. He knew no family life, lived without entertainment, without friends, without companionship. The thought of a wife, a home, or children never crossed his mind. Everything within John was for God. The devotion of an Abraham, of a Moses, of an Elijah, of an Elisha, of an Amos, paled in the presence of this single-minded celibate whose only friend and companion was his Lord.

Never before had the world seen anything like John, nor was it likely to see such a man ever again.

One evening, while standing upon the sandstone cliffs that overlooked the Dead Sea and watching a blazing red sun set behind jagged hills, a voice from heaven spoke to him.

> *"John, the fullness of time has come. What you have lived your entire life for is at hand. Go. Proclaim the Day of the Lord. Pull down the mountains; fill in the valleys; prepare a highway for the*

Messiah. Go, John, now. Look neither to the right nor to the left. Let there be nothing else in your life. No one has ever carried so great a responsibility as do you at this hour.

"Proclaim the coming of the Lord!"

CHAPTER 5

THE NOMADIC CARAVANS WERE the first to come face-to-face with the desert prophet. Their eyes registered unbelief as they gazed upon the sight of such an emaciated creature. Their first thought was simple enough. "He is some madman who wandered into the desert." Or, more charitably, "The heat has driven one of the Essenes quite mad."

Obviously this nameless man was a Jew; but he wore the garment of an unclean animal, the loathsome camel. And it was soon rumored that for food he ate locusts–a food used by only the poorest, most impoverished people.

His outward appearance declared him a lunatic; his words declared him a prophet. His hair, unkempt, reached almost to his knees. His face was that of an old man, but his voice thundered with the vigor of youth. His eyes flashed the burning fire of the desert.

Despite themselves, men could not but stop and stare . . . *and* listen. The voice rang clear. The words were majestic and bold, almost poetic. There was power in every word. The man himself projected a dignity and integrity almost beyond the grasp of human understanding.

The caravans slowed and formed into a circle around the man. Every soul strained to hear what this man had to say.

And what these desert travelers heard resonated with their own deepest feelings. At the same moment, his words convicted each of them. Everything the man spoke was unnerving. What he predicted was impossible, but what he demanded was even more incredulous. John was not only demanding radical change from his hearers, but he was demanding it right there, right then.

No one, they were sure, would take this man seriously.

The caravans would move on, but others would come; and they, too, would stop and listen. And each caravan, when at last it exited the desert, carried with it the reports of a madman or prophet out in the desert, preaching to all who dared paused to hear.

"Why does he not come into the villages to proclaim his message? Does he not know all respectable prophets preach in the marketplaces where people can hear them? Does the fool think people are going to go out there in that infernal hell to hear him? What person in his right mind is going to that pathless wilderness and standing beneath the blistering sun to listen to a man make demands no one is going to respond to. He is mad, all right."

Yet it happened. Some in the caravans, on their return voyage, would search out the desert prophet. Common folk in villages on the edge of the desert made their way out to hear him. Seeking hearts, empty souls, hungry spirits–desperately longing for something they knew they did not have–dared to take their empty lives into that uncharted wasteland to find *The Prophet.*

At first only a few heard him, but they came back to tell their friends of what they had experienced. Rumors about this wildman spread throughout all of Judea and Galilee.

Listeners came first in ones and twos, then by scores and hundreds, and then by thousands. They came on foot, across burning sands. Their numbers grew daily. Some enterprising men were soon scheduling whole caravans into the desert to hear this man.

They all listened. Some wept. Others fell earnestly to their knees. Many cried out in loud voices for undeserved forgiveness. Others cheered. No one jeered. Not a critical word came from any mouth, at least not among the common people.

Yet those who never heard him, who lived in the far-off city of Jerusalem . . . *they* judged him, tried him, and convicted him . . . without having seen nor heard him. The verdict was simple. And familiar. It is laid on every nonconformist of every age. "He has a demon."

A few came and sat down right at his feet. Their purpose was clear: These men wished to be John's disciples. And so it came to be.

This handful of disciples would take on John's lifestyle and become his constant companions. Like him, they would become austere, grave, and humorless men. They would carry within their hearts, as he did in his, the burden of the sins of Israel. These men joined John in his titanic task of preparing the way for the coming of God's own Messiah.

To hear John was to hear the unexpected, for each day was different. Each day John spoke, and each time he spoke he addressed something the crowd had never heard anyone else say. His daring, his fearlessness in broaching any topic, awed the multitude *and* his disciples.

On one particularly hot day, when the crowds seemed to stretch to the horizon, John cried out, "The day after the next Sabbath I will go to the Jordan River. There I will immerse beneath the Jordan waters all who have repented of their way of life. I will immerse all who make their lives ready for the coming of the Lord."

It was on that day John received a new name, a name which was soon to be on the lips of all Israel, for on that day he became known as John the Immerser.

CHAPTER 6

PEOPLE CAME TO HEAR JOHN BECAUSE THEY were seeking something to fill a deep vacancy in their lives.

Merchants came to hear him and repented of their business practices and were then baptized in the fabled waters of the Jordan. Soldiers came, repented of their brutality, and were baptized. The camel drivers came, the farmers, the rustic fishermen, housewives, women of renown, women of the streets, all kinds and all classes came. And all who came, it seemed, came holding some secret sin, repented thereof, and disappeared beneath the Jordan waters.

Every Jew knew the ancient meaning of a soul's being plunged beneath the water of that particular river. It meant the end of life, the cessation of everything. Everyone awaiting baptism stood on the eastern bank, which was a foreign land. There they stepped into the water and disappeared . . . there to die. But each came up out of the water and stepped onto the western bank, safe within the border of the Promised Land, there to begin a new life with God. This simple drama was unforgettable.

There was one particular day at the Jordan that stood out from all others. It began with the arrival of horse-drawn carriages. A delegation of dignitaries had arrived. What important personages had come out to this obscure place?

It was the nation's religious leaders.

When John saw these costumed men, every muscle in his body became motionless. There was not one outer movement on his countenance to betray his inward feelings. As these religious dignitaries cut through the crowd, John watched as ordinary people dropped their heads or genuflected in a gesture of honor. This did not at all set well with the greatest nonconformist of all time.

John read every man as he stepped out of the carriages. Some had obviously come to sneer, to gather evidence against John, and to condemn. Others came with a great deal of uncertainty, hoping to discover for themselves whether or not John was a true prophet. There were even a few among them, the youngest, who came truly believing that John was a man of God. These young men hoped the older, more respected leaders might agree with their unspoken opinion. After all, if the older leaders gave their blessing to John, some of the young men knew they would be free to become his disciples.

But John saw more than this. He looked in the heart of every man now making his way through the midst of the crowd, and discerned the ultimate weakness of each one. There was not *one* among them brave enough, on his own, to break with accepted religious traditions.

The crowd continued giving way before these vaunted leaders. The delegation was on its way to the front of the crowd, to take their rightful place of honor. This was more than the desert prophet could ever hope to stomach. The religious system of his day, coming *here*? And daring to impose their abominable practices *here*? How dare they come! How dare they bring their arrogance, contempt, disdain, and pride to *this* place!

John had not come to this earth to compromise, nor to win over such men to the ways of God. After all, these men saw themselves as authorities in God's ways. John would not attempt to do the impossible: He would not call the leaders of the religious system to come out of that system. Yet the presence of these men was perverting the freedom that the baptized ones had gained as they laid aside the systemization of this world.

John, therefore, declared war. Open, unbridled, unquartered war . . . on Israel's most revered personages. He wanted every human being present to know how he felt about the chains that traditionalists had forged upon the hearts and souls of God's people. And just how did he feel? He felt this whole religious culture must perish.

There was nothing John could do better than thunder, and on this occasion he roared like a lion. Thrusting out the forefinger of one hand, he shattered earth and heaven with his denunciation.

"Who . . . who, I ask . . . who told you to repent?

"You nest of snakes, what are you doing here?"

The crowd was stunned. No one had *ever* talked this way to *these* men. Many in the crowd instinctively rose to their feet; after a moment, wide grins began to appear on the faces of some. But every eye was now riveted on the religious leaders. What would be their reaction? And, was it possible . . . had John committed some kind of blasphemy? The people knew the rumors about John being possessed of a demon; this was not going to help. They loved him for his boldness, yet no one ever dreamed he would take on the religious leaders of their nation. *No one* did that!

Shock turned to disbelief as John continued.

"I ask you again, you nest of snakes, who told you to turn away from the wrath that is coming on you?"

The religious leaders stopped. No one could speak to them in this way. After a brief moment, one of the leaders pulled his cloak up about him, turned, and whispered something to those nearest him. They, in turn, signaled to the others to make a sudden retreat.

But John was not finished.

> *"Your tree! An axe has been laid to your tree. The wrath of God is upon you. The axe will cut down your tree and destroy its root. The day is not far when all that you are shall be destroyed under the wrath of God."*

With that the delegation, as one, gathered up their outer robes and hurried back toward their carriages, each devising in his heart some form of vengeance to take against John.

Someone in the crowd began to cheer. Someone else clapped. With that, the whole multitude stood and took up the applause. Everywhere men and women felt shackles falling from their souls. At last, someone had dared to challenge the religious system!

Spontaneously, the multitude moved toward John. It seemed that every soul present who had not been baptized wanted very much to do so now. They had all, as one, glimpsed something deeper of John's message, something they had never understood before.

It was a glorious day. Yet no one seemed to have laid hold of the obvious. Conduct like this would get John killed.

And then there was that other very memorable day.

CHAPTER 7

THE DOOR FROM THE OTHER REALM OPENED, like a window, just over the Jordan River. Out from the very center of the being of God the Father came forth His own sacred Spirit, the Holy Spirit, somewhat as a dove might, fluttering out through the open door and coming to rest on one of the spectators who was listening to John speak.

John's eyes scanned the crowed, his fierce gaze catching every face. What was that? A light of unnatural origin, appearing out of nowhere, like a dove flying out of a window and coming to rest on someone out there in the crowd.

John realized he was seeing what no other eye could see. This was the sign of the Messiah. John fell silent. His only thought was, "Where landed the lighted dove? *Who* is out there?"

Murmuring whispers swept across the crowd. Many followed John's searching gaze.

Spontaneously, John roared,

"Behold the Lamb of God!

"I am nothing. This man is everything. Look no more to me; look to *him.* As for me, I am not even worthy to stoop down and unlatch the sandals that are on the feet of this one."

The Father seemed to agree. Standing in the door between the two realms, He called out.

"This is my beloved Son in whom I am well pleased."

And as God was pleased, so John was pleased. Nor did it bother John as he watched the multitudes forsake him and begin to follow Jesus. After all, John knew he had come into the world for this very reason.

What John did not know was that the easiest days of his work were now behind him. The harder were yet to come.

CHAPTER 8

"TELL ME OF MY COUSIN," asked John.

"Presently he is in Galilee. He, like you, has twelve disciples; there are also others, perhaps fifty or sixty more, who are always with him. He travels from town to town preaching."

The voice was that of Nadab, a follower of John's who had been in Galilee and witnessed Jesus' ministry.

"On occasions he speaks to large multitudes of people, but most of the time he speaks in someone's home."

"What does he speak about?"

"He mostly tells stories. And many of them have a great deal of humor in them."

Nadab paused. "Teacher, did you know he drinks? I mean, he drinks *wine*! And the twelve, his twelve, they are not like us. They laugh a lot.

"He receives many invitations to banquets. It seems he always accepts. Some say he eats too much and drinks too much or, at least, that his *disciples* do."

John's interest was intent, but his demeanor betrayed no evidence of his inward thoughts. Not one person present had the slightest idea what he thought of Nadab's report. It was a trait of John's that dated back to his childhood.

Nadab continued. "The people he keeps company with are mostly tax collectors, whores, and . . . well, people like that."

One of John's other disciples broke in with an observation. "Teacher, we have fasted almost to the point of starvation. We have prayed until our knees were sore. We follow your example in these things. You fast, you spend your life in prayer, you live a life of great restraint and discipline in all things. Your cousin tells stories, talks of lilies and birds, seeds and sheep, goes to banquets where he eats and drinks. He seems, in general, to be enjoying himself enormously. Some have even called him a drunkard and a glutton. Can you understand why some of us are a little confused?"

After a long pause, it became clear that John would not respond. Finally John took a deep breath and stood. "The people are waiting, and I have something important to say to them."

John walked out into the midst of the gathered multitude and mounted a large stone. It was late afternoon. A cool breeze from the Sea of Galilee was blowing across the field. The sun was setting, and as it did, it bugled enormous golden rays across the sky.

John looked out across the people and called his heart to remember again his life's task: to bring Israel to full repentance, to level mountains, fill in the valleys, and prepare the way for God's final and greatest work upon the earth.

"Our king," cried John, "has taken unto himself his brother's wife. Herod has brought down the wrath of God upon himself. Nor will his wife Herodias be spared."

It would be no later than the next morning when Herod the Tetrarch would hear of John's denunciation. And when Herod heard, he went into a rage. But his rage was nothing compared to that of his new wife, for she vowed the darkest possible vengeance upon John the Baptizer. And in that craving for revenge, she screamed to her husband that John be arrested and thrown into a dungeon. Immediately! Nor did that mark the end of her wicked scheme.

CHAPTER 9

PROTHEUS LOOKED UP TO SEE THE CAUSE of the noise at the top of the stairs. He could make out the shadow of a prisoner standing between two Roman guards. Slowly, laboriously, the shackled prisoner made his way down the long, narrow stairwell.

Protheus could not help but think to himself, "I always imagined you to be a giant of a man; yet here, in this place, you seem in every way to be so ordinary. You appear . . . almost *vulnerable*."

The prisoner now came into full view. Protheus searched John's face, but like so many others, he could find not a single clue in this man's demeanor as to what his thoughts were. Was he afraid? anxious? hostile? Protheus was accustomed to being able to read a prisoner's emotions at this particular moment. But today *this* prisoner provided him nothing.

Protheus turned to one of the soldiers behind him.

"Cell three."

The soldier opened the iron-gated door; just beyond the grating, the cell dropped off into a pit some twelve feet deep. One of the soldiers was about to tie a rope around one of the bars and let himself down into the pit. Protheus interrupted.

"One moment. I will chain the prisoner." With that, Protheus turned to the two Roman guards and motioned for them to unshackle the prisoner. He then walked over to the cell door and let himself down into the rat-infested pit.

The place was dark, wet, and everything else that a dungeon was supposed to be. Protheus called up to the guards. "Step back from the prisoner.

"John, let yourself down here by that rope." John slipped the rope between his hands and lowered himself into the infernal pit.

"These chains fastened to the wall–I must clamp them to your feet and hands. The chains are long enough to allow you some movement. They are ordered from Herod. I am sorry to do this. You will remain in this prison until he decides what to do with you."

For several moments Protheus labored at the task of bolting the iron manacles around John's wrists and ankles. When finished, he stepped back.

"Three of your disciples have asked to see you. They will be allowed to come next week. I understand they are bringing you some food."

Protheus grabbed the rope and was about to pull himself up. He paused, turned, and looked at John full on. "I have heard you speak in the wilderness. I regret . . ."

"It is all right," replied John. "The guilt is not yours."

With that Protheus pulled himself up to the floor above, closed the cell door, and addressed all the soldiers on duty.

"Listen to me. Within whatever bounds that damnable cell affords, you make this man comfortable; supply him with food and water and whatever else he needs. Meet his needs to the limits of the restrictions Herod has placed upon him. One more thing. I have clearly posted John's name on the wall beside his cell door. I want every man in this room to remember who it is in that pit."

A voice called out from the first cell. "What did you say? Have they brought John the Baptist to this place?"

Protheus sighed. He and every other man in the room knew what was coming next.

CHAPTER 10

"HEROD DID IT, DIDN'T HE? That damnable monster.

"John, is that you? Do you remember me? I was with you when you were but a child. Oh, I was a man of greatness then. Look at me now!

"Herod took my home; he took my money. Without a trial, without even a hearing! Then he threw me in this hellhole. Now Herod is the one who is rich! Rich on *my* wealth, and I am but a wretch. I swear a curse upon you, Herod . . . you monster . . . wicked man.

"I served him twenty years. Faithfully. No man has ever lived who has been so unjustly treated as I. It is unfair what he did, I tell you. Now look what that heinous man has done; the ogre has gone out and brought a prophet of God to this cursed place.

"I tell you, every problem, every pain, every sorrow in Judea finds its origin in Herod. There is no justice on this earth, no mercy . . . no pity. It is all his fault. All of it.

"John, can you hear me? Mark my word, you will rot here like the rest of us. Out there in your desert, you said one thing that is true. There is no end to the wickedness of the human heart. And Herod is the worst of all. I would be a happy, prosperous man today if it were not for that cold-blooded Herod, and the others . . . the others . . . *those* wicked men who conspired against me with him to take everything I had."

"Parnach, control your tongue," shouted one of the guards.

There was a pause. The prisoner in the first cell grew quiet. Unfortunately, though, his shouts had awakened the prisoner in the cell next to him.

CHAPTER 11

A THIN, BONY MAN MOVED UP to the door of his cell and looked wildly into the eyes of the captain of the guards.

"John? Here? Are you telling me John is here in the prison of Machaerus? Are you telling me, Protheus, that he has been thrown into cell *three*, of all places?"

"Yes, Hannel, Herod has arrested John and had him brought here."

"Has God no pity? Has God no feelings?" asked Hannel in a cold, thin voice.

"Does devotion mean nothing to Him? *I* once trusted in God, just as John does. Are you really here, John? Do you remember me? I lived a devout and holy life before God. You remember, don't you, John? Well, look at what it has brought me. And you, see what devotion to God has brought *you*? Is this to be the end for men who have loved God and obeyed Him? What kind of a God is it that will allow such things as we now suffer? God, You have thrown one of Your very own servants into a slimy hole!"

Hannel thrust one arm through the bars of his cell, clenched his fist, raised his face, and spat curses at God. He then ended his ravings with one last pronouncement. "Never again will I serve a God who treats men this way. When I needed Him, where was He? John, where is *your* God when you need Him the most?"

Not a single sound rose from the third cell. Whatever John might be thinking, he was keeping his own counsel. Protheus, on the other hand, could not help but wonder: "The prisoner in the first cell blames everything on men. The prisoner in the second cell blames everything on God. I wonder whom the prisoner in the third cell will blame. Man? God?

"Or perhaps his cousin?"

CHAPTER 12

THE SCENE IS A VILLAGE IN GALILEE CALLED NAIN. It is early evening. The streets of the town are packed with people waiting to bring their sick to Jesus.

Some of the infirm are blind, some crippled; one is deaf; another, frothing at the mouth, is held in restraint by his family. An anxious mother holds her small, fevered baby in her arms. Another mother cradles a crippled child in her lap. All manner of people are there, wracked by every disease known to man. All have one thing in common. They are seeking Jesus, hoping to receive healing or liberation at his hands.

The focal point of this crowd is a house located on one of the smaller streets of the village. In every direction the streets leading to this house are jammed with people. Walk through the courtyard and you will see that it, too, is filled.

There is pathos and anxiety everywhere. Perhaps the thing that makes the waiting ones most anxious is to hear a cry of joy coming from within the house and then, a moment later, watch someone depart, praising God for healing.

At this moment, three roughly dressed, leather-skinned men appear at the courtyard gate. One of the disciples of Jesus recognizes these men. He rushes into the house. Just as he is about to tell his master the news of the arrival of these men, a cripple rises on his feet, raises his hands to heaven, and cries out to God in praise for being cured.

"Lord, the disciples of John are here."

Jesus looked up. For one brief moment there was anxiety in his eyes.

"Please. Dismiss the people outside. Bring John's disciples here. Immediately."

With that, the Lord seated himself on the floor and waited pensively for the appearance of John's disciples.

In a moment, the three men solemnly took their place in front of Jesus. There was a long pause. Then Nadab broke the silence.

"We have come from John. He is in prison. Herod had him arrested for . . ."

"Yes, I know," replied the Lord.

"A few days ago we were allowed to visit our teacher. He is chained inside a filthy pit. There are rumors that it will not be long before Herod has him killed."

There was a pause. Nadab waited to see if Jesus had some response to this word.

"John sent us to you, to ask you a question. It was the only request he made of us. We have traveled far to find you, yet it is but for the answer to one question that we come."

Again Nadab paused. Again no one spoke.

"Teacher, the question that John would ask of you is this." Nadab paused again, his face flushed. "John's question is, 'Are you the Messiah, or should we look for another?'"

A long, stunned silence followed. Pain was felt in the heart of every man in the room. You could read it in the faces of John's three disciples, it was evident upon the faces of the twelve, but it was most evident upon the face of the Lord himself.

Jesus sighed deeply. For one brief moment, he dropped his head in what seemed to be a gesture of anguish. Looking up again, he addressed the question.

"Nadab, return to John. Tell him, for me, these things.

"First, tell John that the blind see, the lame walk, and the deaf hear.

"Then tell my cousin that the gospel is proclaimed–not only proclaimed but received with gladness–and that men and women are being set free."

The Lord paused, took a deep, labored breath. Then slowly, purposefully, he continued. "Lastly, Nadab, tell John . . . tell John . . ."

The Lord's voice choked for a moment. Pain was in his words. "Tell my brother John:

"And blessed is he who is not offended with me."

There was another pause. Jesus stood, embraced the three men, and then turned to his disciples. "The hour is very late. It is time we departed here. We must go on to the next village. Please dismiss those waiting outside."

John's three disciples stood, stunned. After a long moment of obvious confusion, they turned and made their departure. The courtyard they crossed was now empty, as were the streets they passed through.

Tomorrow will hold for Jesus yet another village. For the disciples of John, tomorrow will hold the enigma of this day.

But what will tomorrow hold for those who were sent home that evening? They all departed without being healed. And John? What will be his response to the strange words of his cousin?

CHAPTER 13

THE THREE DISCIPLES OF JOHN SQUATTED down on the slimy floor of the dungeon that had become John's home.

"Teacher, we have seen your cousin."

"Did you ask my question?"

"We did."

"And his answer?"

"Teacher, the answer is very strange. We do not understand it."

John sighed. It was as though he knew this would be Nadab's response.

"His reply?"

"Teacher, he said to tell you that the blind and the dumb and the crippled receive sight and hearing and healing. Then he said to tell you that the good news is proclaimed, and received with joy."

John turned those words over in his mind very slowly. After several minutes, his brow wrinkled. The prisoner leaned forward and asked, "Is that all?"

"No, teacher, he said one other thing, and then he dismissed the crowd and bade us farewell. What he said was, 'Tell John, "And blessed is he who is not offended with me."'"

There was a long silence as three men studied the face of John, hoping to glimpse his reaction to these words. But, as always, there was none.

Finally John queried: "Where was my cousin?"

"In a village in Galilee, called Nain," responded Nadab. "There were sick people everywhere; streets, lanes, and alleys were all filled with people wanting to be healed. The place was overrun with suffering souls."

"Were they being healed?"

"Yes, teacher, many were being healed."

With those words, John's interest quickened, his frame straightened. "Did you say, *many*?" responded John.

"Yes, teacher, many."

"Many?" asked John again.

Nadab was puzzled. "Yes, teacher," he answered again, "*Many* were being healed."

"Many," repeated John quietly as to himself. Then he leaned forward again. "Many, Nadab? Many, but *not* all?"

For a brief instant Nadab was at a loss as to what John was saying. Then his own eyes lit up, revealing the shock of what John was observing. "Yes, teacher, you are right. There were many who were being healed, but not *all.*"

". . . *not* . . . all."

John stared vacantly into space. Had he at last found the answer to the questions which had troubled him so deeply about Jesus? Or had he simply added more questions to his dilemma?

At that very moment, there was someone else who was struggling with this same dilemma.

CHAPTER 14

"LEAVE ME," SAID JESUS TO HIS COMPANIONS.

With those words, Jesus wandered off to a sequestered place to be alone. Never before in all his thirty-one years, nor in all his preexistence in eternity, had he ever longed so intensely to answer the cry and the question of someone struggling to understand the mysterious ways of his God.

If ever there was a time for him to give a clear answer, if ever there was a person to whom he should speak clearly, surely the time was now and the person, John. If any man ever lived who had a right to have an explanation given to him, that man was his own flesh and blood, his only cousin.

"John, your pain is great. I feel it. Tonight you so desperately need to understand me, to fathom my ways, to peer into the riddle of my sovereignty. Your heart is breaking. But, John, you are not the first to have this need. You are but one in a long train of humankind stretching across all the centuries of man who have called out to me with questions and doubts. You are but one voice among so many who wonder and who agonize over my ways."

With those words spoken, a scene of an event that had taken place long ago began to emerge before the eyes of the Lord.

Jesus shuddered. Before him was Egypt. The Lord of time stepped into the streets of the city of Pharaoh. "I have been here before. I have walked down these streets, listening to the quiet cries, the murmurings, the prayers of my own people . . . held here in slavery."

The Lord paused and looked about. He could clearly hear every prayer being prayed. They seemed to be lifted up to him in harmony with their rustling chains.

"You who are descendants of a man named Jacob, you have cried out to me so long, suffered so long, and wept so long. You have lifted your faces to heaven for years without number. But the heavens are stone. It appears your God has gone deaf. You have been born in slavery. You have grown up, cried out for freedom, and then died, without your prayers being answered. Your children came along to take your place, were fettered with the same worn chains of their fathers. They, too, cried out for deliverance, and they, too, died with their chains still forged to their wrists."

The Lord walked on.

"Your children's children have grown old. They have come to me with their prayers myriads of times, calling out, 'God deliver us from the Pharaoh, deliver us from this slave master who does not know our father, Joseph. Oh, our God, lead us back to our homeland.'

"But I did not answer, not so much as one word. And so it continued for you and your offspring . . . for twelve generations.

"I left you in slavery for almost four hundred years. Never once in all that time were your prayers answered. You cried out to me, but I did not respond. No clear word, no insight into my ways, no explanation of my purposes, no reasons were given why I did not answer your cries. Your hearts were broken before me.

"But my heart was broken with yours.

"After four hundred years, there were still men and women who were believing in me! After four hundred years of not hearing from me, still you believed!"

At that moment came a piercing cry. It was the voice of a mother.

"Oh, God, if You are there, will You not answer? Tomorrow this beautiful child will be taken from my arms, forever. He will be shackled, enslaved, and forever doomed to make bricks beside the river Nile. I will die never to see my child again. He will grow old and die in the chains they forge upon his wrists tomorrow. Will You not hear my cry?"

The eyes of the Lord filled with tears.

"Oh, Israel, you are confronted with one simple fact.

"Oh woman, you, like all those before you . . . you, like my cousin John, rotting in a pit . . . have come face to face with one stark truth.

"Your God has not lived up to your expectations."

CHAPTER 15

THE SCENE CHANGED. Once more the place was Egypt, but it was many years into the future. On this occasion, the Lord of time stepped into an unfolding drama that was a scene, not of slavery, but of death.

Women were frantically running down the streets, with Egyptian solders in pursuit. Every newborn Hebrew male child would be slain that day. That is, all but one. The one lone survivor would grow up to save Israel from Egypt. But these panic-stricken mothers did not know this. They would live out their entire lives without even one of them ever knowing that eighty years hence God would avenge the death of their children and set Israel free.

"They do not know," he sighed. "They *will* know, but not here on this earth. All they will ever know in this lifetime is that I did not come to them in their hour of greatest need. Today they, like all others, have met a God they do not understand.

"So it has been in all the past, so it will be throughout all ages to come."

The scene changed again. The Lord of space and time was back in Galilee again, alone. Once more he spoke.

"If I ever cared for those who lived in slavery in Egypt; if I ever cared for Job on his ash heap, or Jeremiah in his miry pit; if I ever cared for my people when the armies of Nebuchadnezzar surrounded Jerusalem and carried them off to slavery; if I ever longed to give answer and explanation; if there were one day above all others that I would speak, today would be that day.

"This day I have flesh and blood. I have a human mother who loved Elizabeth and who loves Elizabeth's son. She does not wish to see him die, and like all others, she wants so much to understand. Today I have brothers; I have sisters. I am an earthen man, with blood coursing through my veins, with human emotions, with family responsibilities. John and I are the elder sons of our two families. It is with human eyes I watch this unholy deed of Herod. Nor is that all. Everywhere I look I see my people caught up in circumstances not of their own making.

"If ever there has been a moment I have longed to answer the questions of any man or woman, it is now. And it is to you, John, I want to give an explanation of my ways.

"John, I watched you walk into that desert as a twelve-year-old child. I saw your days turn to weeks and your weeks turn into years, as you fasted, as you ate the scraps of the desert, as you clothed yourself with the desert's waste. I have watched your soft skin turn to leather. I have seen you age inordinately. Your faithfulness to me is without parallel. Not since Eve bore her first man-child has there ever been one like unto you.

"I gave you a task greater than the one I gave to Moses. You are a prophet greater than any who has ever come before.

"But, most of all, you are my kin. You are my own flesh and blood.

"If ever, ever I have wanted to give answer to a man's questions, to explain my sovereign ways, it is today. Yet I have been to you, as to all others, a Lord *not* fully understood, a God who rarely makes clear exactly what He is doing in the life of one of His children.

"Angels shall plea
to set thee free,
Death shall weep
when he comes for thee,
Yet ne'er shall an answer come
from me."

CHAPTER 16

AS DAY DAWNED IN THE VILLAGE OF NAIN, the multitude that had gathered there the night before received an unbearable shock. Jesus had departed the village the night before, soon after he dismissed the crowd for the evening. He was gone, and *no* one knew where.

That morning a mother, who had come all the way from Damascus carrying her crippled child, would begin the long trek back home, still carrying a beloved child with a never-to-be-healed twisted foot. Throughout all the rest of her long life this mother would wonder why the Lord had not waited just a few more moments before dismissing the crowd, for she was next in line.

"And blessed are you
if you are not offended with me."

That same morning, an old man was guided back to his home by a friend, there to ever wonder, until the day he died, what sight might have been like if only he had been able to reach the master healer just a few minutes earlier. But his destiny would forever be a life of darkness . . . and wondering.

"And blessed is he
who is not offended with me."

A mother will return home with her young daughter who will forever remain disfigured because of a childhood accident. Throughout that despondent day and on into the following weeks and years, that mother will look down into the face of her child and often hear her ask why she was not healed that day in Galilee. "After all, Mother, so many others were."

The mother will give first one answer and then another; those answers will satisfy neither mother nor daughter. Both will forever wonder why the Lord left them that evening, not caring enough for them to remain just a little longer. The mother will die and go to her grave; her daughter will grow up to womanhood carrying her disfigurement throughout her life.

"And blessed is that one
who is not offended with me."

A sick baby will die. An epileptic child will go on having seizures as long as he lives. A fevered young girl will suffer weeks of pain before she regains her health. A deaf mute will spend the rest of his life begging at the city gate. These and many others, with even more tragic stories, departed the village of Nain that morning . . . each so downcast that words could not express their feelings of hopelessness. Worst of all, from God came no explanation concerning His ways.

Many were healed. But not all.

"And blessed is he
who is not offended with me."

CHAPTER 17

PROTHEUS PUSHED OPEN THE HEAVY prison door and stepped out into the sunlight to escape the stench of the dungeon and, for a moment, to breathe fresh air. Immediately the music from Herod's palace caught his ear. Herod was giving a huge banquet for his friends that evening. "Honoring his own birthday!" recalled Protheus. There would be revelry. There would be . . .

Suddenly a cold chill gripped Protheus.

It would be just like Herod . . . to haul John the Baptist up to the banquet hall to make sport of him!

"That is exactly what he will do."

Protheus whirled around and rushed back into the prison. . . . He wanted to warn John about what might happen to him before the evening was over. But before he could reach John's cell, Protheus felt a strong hand on his shoulder. He turned. It was one of Herod's personal bodyguards.

"It's John, is it not? You have come for John. Herod is going to make sport of him."

"Far worse than that," replied the bodyguard, betraying his own apprehension. "Far, far worse than that. Salome, the daughter of Herod's wife, has just danced for the guests. Herod is drunk, and in his stupor he offered Salome anything she wanted, up to half his kingdom. She, in turn, inquired of her mother just what to ask for in the presence of so lucrative an offer." The bodyguard paused.

"Protheus, it seems that tonight Herod's guests will *not* be entertained by making sport of John the Baptist. No, it will be far more macabre than that. John's head is to be brought into the banquet room on a platter!"

Protheus lost his balance; his eyesight blurred. The bodyguard grabbed his arm and steadied him. "The same thing happened to me when I heard," observed the guard.

"What now?" asked Protheus.

"I would say John has less than five minutes to live. Bring him to me."

"May the gods have mercy on us," whispered Protheus. "And if there be but one God, and if that God be the God of the Jews, we would be fools to believe He would show pity on us for what we are about to do."

CHAPTER 18

"JOHN, THEY HAVE COME FOR YOU. Much sooner than you had thought. In a few minutes you will be no more. There is no time to send word to your disciples. Nor to my mother, Mary, who has worried so much for your safety. You will not be given opportunity of even a single word to anyone. Nor will you be able to ask again the question you addressed to me.

"In less than four minutes now, you will be dead. How many thoughts can be crowded into one's mind in four minutes? How many doubts? How many questions? Not many. But, John, worst of all, there will be *no* answers.

"And blessed are you, John,
if you are not offended with me.

"They have unshackled you. The staircase is before you. The door above is open. You can see the light of day above you.

"Why is this happening to you, John? You, of all people? Your head . . . *severed* from your body? Why? Because of an obscene dance by a teenage girl. How ironic.

"You will never live to see your thirty-third birthday, nor will you know exactly why I have called you. Nor will you know if your life on this earth counted for anything. Those long years in the searing desert, you denied yourself of everything this earth affords except food and water, and only enough of that to keep you alive. You did this all for me. Yet, as you face death, there is no evidence that your life was anything but wasted. Have I forsaken you in the hour you need me most?

"And blessed are you
if you are not offended with me.

"You have reached the head of the stairs. You are not sure which way they would have you turn. A guard points to the left. You follow. Is this happening? You have less than one minute before that immutable blank. You recall those long vigils before my face. Did you misunderstand me? Were you mistaken? Perhaps you did not hear my voice at all?

"In all those years you lived alone in the desert you never once knew love or comfort from another human being. Will I not extend such comfort to you now, at last? You never had the pleasure of your own children to climb up on your lap, to give you earthly joy. You never came in contact with a woman, ever; you never had a wife. You have never known intimate love. You have never even had a friend. Your whole life was lived for your calling, and for me. Will I not now, in this last moment of your life, part the veil and allow you to see something . . . anything . . . of my purpose in your life and in your death? You will die wondering why I ate and drank as I did, why I did not fast as you fasted, nor pray as you prayed. Was the Messiah not to be a man of sorrows and acquainted with grief?

"You will die today at the hands of unclean, uncircumcised,

heathen, Gentile Romans. But your death at their hands will come about only by my sovereign permission. And you will die not understanding why I allowed this seemingly senseless act.

"And blessed are you
if you are not offended with me.

"You will not see the multitudes cry out in jubilation at my entry into Jerusalem. Neither will you see me crucified, nor hear of my resurrection and my triumph over death. You will die not knowing that you have proclaimed the coming of no less than the *Son of God.*

"Death is but a few seconds away, and still there is no answer to your question. You will die not understanding.

"And blessed are you, John,
if you are not offended with me.

"They have opened the gate to the courtyard. There it is, the block on which you will lay your head, and there the man who will take your life. You will be remembered as one of the greatest men who ever lived. But you will not know that, nor will you hear the Son of God say, 'Of men born of women, there was none greater than John.'

"Even now as you kneel, you wonder if you are a complete failure. You gave so much, poured out your life so completely, lived for God so singularly. Yet, despite all this, you could not so much as win the favor of God to the point of His giving you one answer to one question. It was, after all, the only request you ever made.

"I did not give to you an answer. I never have. The question of *why* always remains unanswered in all my dealings with men; this is my way. But if there were one human being on this earth to whom I would make clear my purpose, it would be *you.* And it would be now. Above all other men or women who have ever lived, I would give an answer to *you.*"

John knelt and placed his head upon the block.

"When I called you, John, and told you that you would announce the coming of the Messiah, you assumed that because you were going to prepare the way for me, you would have the joy of seeing that wonderful day of my coming in glory. But today you have met a God you do not understand. Such is the mystery of my sovereignty. Such are my ways in *every* generation. No man has ever understood me, not fully. No man ever will. I will always be something other than what men expect me to be. I will work out my will in ways different from what men foresee.

"The guard has shifted his weight. The blade is raised above you. Death stands beside you. Die, my brother John, in the presence of a God who did not live up to your expectations.

"And blessed are you
if you are not offended with me."

Shall we scorn that God has revealed
so little concerning His ways, or rejoice
that He has revealed so much?

CHAPTER 19

A DAY LIKE THAT WHICH AWAITED JOHN awaits us all. It is unavoidable because every believer imagines his God to be a certain way, and is quite sure his Lord will do certain things under certain conditions. But your Lord is never quite what you imagined Him to be.

You have now come face to face with a God whom you do not fully understand. You have met a God who has not lived up to your expectations. Every believer must come to grips with a God who did not do things quite the way it was expected.

You are going to get to know your Lord by faith or you will not know Him at all. Faith in Him, trust that is in *Him* . . . *not* in His ways.

Today you are resentful of those who so callously hurt you. But no, not really. The truth is you are angry with God because, ultimately, you are not dealing with men, you are dealing with the sovereign hand of your Lord. Behind all events, behind all things, there is always His sovereign hand.

The question is not, "Why is God doing this? Why is He like this?" The question is not, "Why does He not answer me?" The question is not, "I need Him desperately; why does He not come rescue me?" The question is not, "Why did God allow this tragedy to happen to me, to my children, to my wife, to my husband, to my family?" Nor is it, "Why does God allow injustices?"

The question before the house is this: "Will you follow a God you do not understand? Will you follow a God who does not live up to your expectations?"

Your Lord has put something in your life which you cannot bear. The burden is simply too great. He was never supposed to do *this*! But the question remains, "Will you continue to follow this God who did not live up to your expectations?"

"And blessed are you
if you are not offended with me."

Epilogue

"CAPTAIN, THE THIRD CELL IS EMPTY."

"It will not be empty long. I have just received word that we are to receive a new prisoner."

"What has this one done?"

"I do not know. There is always the possibility this one is as innocent as was John."

The soldier's response was simple. "I hate having such prisoners! We have a prisoner in the first cell who rails against unfairness, against men, and against circumstances. We have a prisoner in the second cell who is hostile toward God because of what his God has done to him. . . ."

"The new prisoner has arrived," called a voice at the head of the stairs.

"Take the rope," said Protheus to the guard. "Lower the prisoner into the miry pit."

Who is this prisoner? Who is this one who will now be imprisoned in the third cell? What name will be inscribed beside the cell door?

One thing is certain: It was inevitable that this person be sent here. Inevitable, unavoidable, and a sovereign act of God.

The prisoner's name? Surely, the question is not necessary, dear reader; *you* are the prisoner in the third cell!

"And blessed are you
if you are not offended with me."

"Cousin?"

"Yes, John."

"Jesus?"

"Yes, John. It is I."

"My Lord and my God . . . but I had so many questions as I faced death!"

"So did I when I faced death. Just as I did not answer you, neither did my Father answer me. We died in quite similar ways."

"You died? You died as ignominiously, as I did?"

"Yes, John. But I rose from the dead."

"You rose from the dead? But how?

"Come, brother John . . . take my hand. The moment has come. I will now take you to that place where you know . . . even as you are known."

Dear reader, no one can fully understand the pain you feel as you suffer your present situation. Whether it came upon you because of circumstances or by the deeds of men, one thing is certain. Before this present tragedy entered into your life, it first passed through the sovereign hand of God.

"And blessed are you . . ."

Book Discussion Guide

1. Look at pages 121–123, which describe John's absolute devotion to God, unimpeded by cares of this world. What would you require, or what thorns would you need to pull from your life (see Luke 8:14), to live unhindered before God?

2. We remember John for many things, not least Jesus' praise in Matthew 11:11: "Of all who have ever lived, none is greater than John the Baptist." But in this story, John never felt his ministry was great. What's your opinion of your own legacy? How do you expect people will remember you?

3. How do you generally react to nonconformists–people who don't fit in by nature or by choice? How does your immediate community respond to them? How welcome are they in your church?

4. How can we recognize a person of God? What are the hallmarks to look for, and how can we avoid looking at the wrong factors?

5. John railed against the Pharisees, who had burdened the people with man-made religious rules. Are there any religious or social systems today that might prevent people from

connecting with God? What can you do to change or oppose those systems?

6. John answered God's calling and, though he had questions, never looked back. What is God calling you to do? How can you be wholehearted?
7. Has God ever failed to meet your expectations? How did you respond to Him? What happened in your relationship with Him as a result?
8. Why did Hannel and Parnach land in the first and second cells? How did they respond to their predicaments? What is your response when you face adversity or trouble?
9. When John's disciples brought his question to Jesus (pages 144–145), what caused Jesus such anguish? Do you think Jesus has ever had a similar response to your own doubts or anxious fears?
10. Reread chapter 16. How do you respond to a God we do not understand, who is capable of healing many but does not heal all? Have you ever been offended with God? If so, what are the standards to which you were holding God? Why do you think He remains so difficult to understand?
11. Think of a time when you've prayed or pleaded and the only answer has been silence. How did this affect your relationship with God? What do you think God was saying by remaining silent?
12. "I will always be something other than what men expect me to be. I will work out my will in ways different from what men foresee" (page 164). Do you agree with the author's proposition? What can we know of God? What sort of assumptions about Him should we avoid?
13. Do you trust your understanding of God, or do you trust God Himself (chapter 19)? When is it easy to confuse the two?

THE DIVINE ROMANCE

Imagination has always had
power of resurrection
that no science can match.
INGRID BENGIS

With deepest affection

to my oldest daughter,

Lynda

* * *

Above all temples
You chiefly prefer
Oh Spirit
The heart upright
and pure.

Instruct me
You who know
For You were present
from the first.

You sat
dove like
With might
and outspread wings
Brooding over
the vast abyss
And made
it pregnant.

Oh Spirit
what in me
Is dark
Illumine.

The prayer of John Milton as he took up his pen to write Paradise Lost

It has been my fondest hope that we might meet again. When last we met it was a drama that we viewed together.

On this occasion, it is a love story. Of all love stories, I find this one unequaled. I trust, at story's end, you might share that view with me.

The places reserved for us are box seats. We shall have what I hope will be the best possible view of this unfolding saga.

Let us hasten in, now, as I see the ushers are about to close the doors. This is not a thing we would want to miss.

Prologue

He was alone.

The first tick of time had never sounded, nor had the unending circle of eternity yet commenced. There were neither things created nor things uncreated to share space with him. He dwelt in an age before the eternals, where all there was . . . was God. Nor was there space for anything else. He was the uncreated. He was the ALL.

In this non-time of so long ago, there was but one life form . . . the highest life.

He was also love.

Passionate, emotional, expressive . . . love.

In this God, dwelling so all alone, there was a paradox: though he was alone, he was also love. Yet there was no *counterpart* for him to love. A love so vast, so powerful, yet, there was no "other than."

Then life pulsated, light blazed in newfound glory as revelation ascended in him, as he cried from within the council of the Godhead.

There can be ***two!***

"I . . . the living God . . . shall have a *counterpart!*"

Exulting in revelation, he consecrated his whole being to this one task: to have . . . *a bride.* For one brief moment the infinite solitude retreated.

But just before he launched his grand design, a very mysterious thing took place *in* God. Deep within the center of his being there occurred an event that no other eye was to see, no other mind to conceive.

A thousand million portions of God burst upward in light. Each of these portions of God ignited into flaming brilliance . . . as if to proclaim that each had been chosen–even *marked off*–for some special, distant destiny. Having marked off these future destinies, the Living God gave himself to making real his highest dream. Unending self-containment would end.

And so he spoke. "Let there *be* . . ."

In so speaking, he relinquished being the All, making room for something other than the All of God. For one brief moment, there was God *and* a great abyss of nothingness.

Never before, and only once since, has there been such a radical change in the history of God. Now, as "Let there be . . ." sounded across the sphere of nothingness, there came a blinding flash that filled that hollow void. Suddenly there was not only the uncreated God . . . there was now something *created!*

Created *light.* A *picture* of God now shared space with God.

He then created a realm of spirituals. Unmeasured, immeasurable, this realm, like its God, fell *outside* all finite understandings, yet this invisible, spiritual sphere was *inside* him. He called it the heavenly places. Though it was a place *in* him, yet it pleased him to enfold himself and dwell there.

He then created living creatures! He called them messengers. These beings were covered in light that emanated from their spirits, just as their God is covered in the glory of the light of his own being.

His messengers were like him in many ways, but they were also unlike him. They were powerful, but not *all* powerful. They were everlasting, but not eternal. (Unlike God, who moved about at will in eternity past, eternity present, and eternity future, they moved only forward, into eternity future.) They had no counterpart, but they had one another for companionship. But these messengers were entirely *unlike* God in one way. They were *neuter.* He was male. And they could not love. They could *glory*, yes! But they could not love . . . *not* as he loved.

And though he joyed in having these creatures present with him, and though his solitude had at last been broken, *they* had one another. Like had like; kind had kind. But for him, there was no kind after *his* kind.

Speaking aloud once more, the Lord called out to the abyss of nothingness, and nothingness gave way to something. . . . A *visible* realm now burst forth from his word.

He spoke again, and at his word this visible realm swarmed with sparkling lights and circling orbs.

He then stretched forth his hand, and there dropped from his fingertips a small and shapeless mass. "Upon this small grain I shall labor, for it is the place of my supreme purpose in creating."

As he worked, the void mass began to take on symmetry. As he labored, he filled the little ball with things never before imagined.

By the sixth day, the small planet swarmed with wonders. His audience, the accompanying angels, watched him create a wholly different life from them–visible life that could hear, that could fly, that could run, that could even cry aloud. But the most startling sight upon the blue-green ball was this: Everything was *two.*

Furthermore, an astonishing kind of *two* it was! Not one of these creatures was neuter. They were male–that is, *half* were male! The most incomprehensible wonder in the universe was *the other half*! These beings were not neuter, and they were not male. They were something *new* and beyond all comprehension! They were female! Male had a counterpart. Kind after his kind. Counterparts.

Here was a concept so wondrous that angels spoke of it in hushed reverence, and staring in pristine innocence at their God, they wondered what had provoked him to create living things that came in twos . . . each *he* having a *she!*

And so they stared, and so they wondered, and so they viewed these newly created things, saying,

Like us they live and move.
Like us they have kind of their kind.
But, oh, unlike us
They are visible.
Unlike God or angels,
Each has a counterpart.

And they took note, that now *all* living things had *someone else* . . . except One. God was still . . . alone.

PART 1

CHAPTER 1

THE SIXTH DAY OF CREATION WAS drawing to a close. The Lord had grown quite weary; therefore, the angels were quite surprised to see him plunge into a final act of creation.

"You will clearly grasp what I am about to do, for you are the highest form of life in the *unseen* realm, the supreme creation within the invisibles."

He paused, reached down, and scooped up a small handful of earth. He stared at the soil for a moment, then spoke again.

"From this red dirt I will create the highest form of life within the realm of things *visible*. The creature I am about to bring forth will rule over the material universe just as *I* rule over the spiritual universe."

With those words spoken, the Lord God began to shape, mold, and model the red dirt.

The angels watched, and as they did they whispered to one another. "This one shall be as God is . . . a *he*."

They stared, enthralled, at their Lord's intensity. They noted how deeply the aloneness, so uniquely his, was etched upon his face.

Suddenly, the look on the face of the Creator changed. He was searching for something . . . something in his own being. Slowly he drew that element from out of himself and engraved it upon the clay.

With the last sculpting stroke, he stepped back from the moist sod, allowing the angels to have a full view of his completed work. They gasped in amazement and cried together,

His image! Visible!

CHAPTER 2

ONCE MORE THE LORD GOD BENT gently over the sculptured clay. For a moment the face of the Living God and the face carved upon the lifeless clay almost touched.

The Lord God breathed.

Clay nostrils quivered and flared. The wet clay fleshed, stiffened, stirred, and began quietly breathing.

Almost pensively the Lord stepped back. The newest of his creations turned his head . . . and stared for a brief moment at the panorama of celestial beings gathered about. Then, in the most natural of gestures, the rouge-tinted man sat up . . . turned . . . and serenely faced his Sculptor.

With that the Lord approached the model. Again their two faces almost touched, while angels whispered their approval.

"Why, why . . . they are almost like . . . brothers."

Of all the innumerable creatures fashioned by his poetic hand, there was but one of whom it could be said, "The Lord God was thinking of *himself* when he created *this* one."

And, as the angels had surmised, this latest and final creation was male. Not an *it*, therefore not of the angelic species. Visible, therefore of the material realm, yet a far higher form of life than any other being that dwelt in realms visible.

As the angels stood in wonder at this one, the truth declared itself: This creature would rule the earth . . . as surely as the Lord God, in whose image he was so obviously created, rules the heavenlies.

Further, it was noted, this creature–unlike visible animals and invisible angels, but very like God–could love.

And like God, the one called man had no *kind* after his *kind.* Man joined his God as one of but two living things that could love–yet who had no "other" upon whom to pour out that love. Of all the created beings, man was the only male who had no counterpart.

Truly, man was the image of God.

CHAPTER 3

THE SEVENTH DAY WAS A DAY of rest for all creation. The highest activity of the day reached no higher than wonderment.

The eighth day dawned. It was the second *first* day of the week. For the Lord God, this day was to be a day spent in fellowship with his image. It was obvious that they enjoyed one another's company above all others'.

Together the two traversed man's terrestrial domain, wandering across the face of that emerald ball, roaming meadows, valleys, hills. Together they drank in earth's beauty and absorbed its windsong.

And as they went, first one, then the other, would declare, "Ah, this is good."

"Yes, and this . . ."

"And this, too, is good."

But as the day progressed, the conduct of the man became disturbingly strange. He would fix his penetrating gaze upon some distant, misty object and then suddenly bound his way toward it, only to find the lion, the leopard, or the eagle. For a moment his discovery caused his face to fall. He would then slowly turn and murmur, in a pathos that could disquiet a seraph, "Two. They are always two."

The deep restlessness of the man intensified. At length this disquietude of man was addressed by his Lord.

"You have seen a goodly portion of all my creation, and you have seen the portion I have given you to rule. Is there *anything* in all this vast realm which, to your observation, might *not* be good?"

Slowly, and with the greatest deliberation, man cast his eye over his vast and lush domain. The verdict was incontestable. All was good.

Yet, not all.

There was something amiss deep within the man. Something he could not define . . . yet it was there, and he strove to identify it. A silent cry arose from within and chilled his being to the core.

He again faced his Creator, fixing a steady gaze upon the blazing fires within the eyes of God. Neither spoke while eyes exchanged a consortium of emotions–the mutual loneliness, the shared sadness that they alone, among all living things, had touched.

The Lord at last broke the spell of silence.

"Let us see, for a certainty, if all things in my creation are good."

Man, by some spiritual instinct of his inner nature, knew that he was now to call forth all the creatures of earth and name each of them.

The animals came forth, always in pairs, each with his counterpart. The lion pranced before man with his lioness; the proud stallion and the mare; the bull, the cow. Two, always two.

"What is amiss here?" A wild look grew in his eyes as he cried out, "I am Ish! Man! Ruler of this domain. But alone. One, only. Where is *my* counterpart?"

The last pair of animals passed. Man looked frantically about, then broke into a run across valleys and hills until he came to the precipice of a great mountain and began searching the horizon.

"Are you there?" he called. "Are you there?"

He scoured the whole terrestrial ball, then searched the moon and stars above. Slowly, silently, he made his way back into the valleys and to a waiting and very understanding God. Man again fixed his troubled eyes upon the blazing fire within the eyes of God.

"What is it that is not good?" asked Adam.

"I believe you know. Man, it is not good for you to be alone."

For a long time, the young man and a God not old shared in their spirits what no words, mortal or divine, could ever express.

"You are my image. Male. Alone. And it is not good for you to be thus," said the Lord very quietly.

Man searched out the face of God for a long time before he replied.

"I am, as you are. Alone!"

CHAPTER 4

UNMINDFUL OF PATH OR HOUR, the man began to wander . . . without purpose or direction. The unbearable ache within his heart throbbed on. His senses revealed to him the harsh truth. "I am more alone than if I were the only living creature in all realms." Time unmeasured passed. At last, worn and forlorn, he wandered back to his Creator.

"You are true, as truth you are," spoke the man as he approached a God whom he now better understood. "But is there no deed, no act, of God or man that might bring forth . . . my Ishah? Even for one brief moment, to see, to touch–something . . . someone . . . like unto me? May I not, even for an hour, have *my* lioness?"

The Lord heaved a deep sigh as one about to begin a great and arduous task. "Man, there is a principle written within the depths of my being that cannot be rescinded."

"I am one, not two. Indivisible is my life. And you, man, are a reflection of my essence. Therefore, one also are you. As I am alone, so are you alone. As indivisible am I, so indivisible are you. More than one you cannot be. To change that is to violate the reflection of me, which reflection you are."

Upon hearing this inexorable verdict, a flawless man, standing in the midst of a flawless universe, began to weep. For the first time creation witnessed the exquisite agony of tears of sorrow.

Man raised his face and, speaking between sobs, said, "You are very much like me, are you not?"

"No, not at all," came the Lord's gentle reply. "*You*, man, are very much like me."

As the full meaning of these words slipped into his soul, the man dropped to his knees, his unspeakable sorrow finding expression only in uncontrollable sobs.

At last the man grew still, lifted his face of blended tears and pain to his Maker, and spoke again, in words of grim finality. "There is, then, no way. As you are, so I am destined ever to be."

An overwhelming heart of love and a life lived out in solitude now found a hesitant voice and measured words:

Perhaps, my image,
perhaps
there is
a way.
But only one.

The Creator reached down to the soil and plucked forth a *seed*. For an endless moment, the man watched his Lord stare silently and sadly at the seed.

Slowly the Lord God held out the seed for the man to see.

"Here is yet another principle, buried deep within my nature. This principle, therefore, is found also in the very fiber and bloodstream of the universe. Even in *you*, man. 'Tis a law of my nature, not known to my creation, yet this principle lives also within this small, terrestrial seed. Like us, this simple seed is alone. And–like us–it must *forever* abide . . . alone."

"Forever? . . . my Lord, my God . . . alone . . . *forever*?"

"Yes, man . . . forever . . . *unless* . . ."

"Unless what?" cried the man at this faint hint of hope. "Tell me! Unless *what*!"

"Unless . . ." The Lord paused.

"In the name of pity, unless what!"

The answer came quietly and evenly. "Unless, perchance, the seed should fall into the ground and there cease its existence." With that, the Lord dropped the seed into the earth.

Man rushed to the site of the burial and exclaimed, "But I cannot fall into the ground and cease to exist." He paused, lowered his voice and added, "That is . . . well . . . I cannot, can I?"

The Lord turned and, gazing into some far distant age, murmured, "Perhaps–perhaps one day such a thing might come to pass."

"But," interrupted the still-agitated man, "what would be the good of it?" He stared again at the moist sod. "For what gain would it be if *I* should disappear forever into the earth? Then, should my counterpart appear, my *counterpart* would be *alone*."

"Have you not observed, man–and I believe you have–that eventually the seed *rises* again. It rises from the captivity of its earthen chamber. And, having risen, the seed is no more *one* seed. And no longer alone. The seed is *many*.

"Yet I tell you a mystery. The seed is still . . . *one*."

The man stood almost motionless, fixing his eyes first on the earth and then on the face of God. Slowly, but with rising expectation, he replied,

All I have heard
I do not fully see.
Your thoughts are beyond
those bestowed on me.
Your sight is not mine to own.

Nor angels nor archangels, I presume,
have ever known this thought.
But this I declare,
Make me a seed!
Place me now, this hour,
into that dirt
from which I sprang.
Out from your finger
or out from my heart
bring forth to me now
my counterpart.

These words seemed to end, for the Creator, some eternal vigilance of waiting.

"You, my very image, are willing to fall, like this singular seed, into the earth that you might thereby end your journey of solitude? You are willing to do *this* to gain a life from your life? You could fall into the earth and cease to exist in order to become as this seed—*many.* You are willing to do this to have a counterpart?"

The man turned to face his God and exclaimed in a voice of unequivocal certainty.

"I am! I am!"

The Lord God lifted first his eyes, then his hand toward the heavenly realms. The celestial response was immediate.

The heavenly host bolted forth into realms visible. A wild, joyous, and expectant throng they were, encircling their Creator and his highest creation. Soon the two were surrounded with angelic light and praise. In the midst of this celestial demonstration the Lord raised his hand again and roared forth a most thunderous and uninhibited declaration.

"For man," he shouted. "For man, I shall now build a counterpart. Kind after his kind!"

The praise vanished. Stunned, the angelic host stood silent.

These were words they did not understand. What God had suggested, they knew full well, was quite impossible.

"This is the eighth day, is it not?" inquired the angels of one another.

"Indeed, it is the eighth day, not the sixth."

"And our Lord declared creation and all creating to have ended on the sixth day, did he not?"

"Can a male bear a child?" came an angelic whisper as yet another probed his inmost being for revelation.

How can the image of God be two, *when God is* one? was the unanswered, unspoken question, burning in the spirits of all the angels.

The Lord turned to face the red-tinted creature standing beside him, that he might answer for them these unanswerable questions.

"You are of the earth. From this very soil I brought you forth, but *not* from this soil shall I bring your counterpart." The Lord paused. Every angel leaned forward. "No, not from the soil . . . but from here!"

Every eye, human and angelic, followed the finger of God. A muffled gasp arose from each and all. The Lord's finger was now, quite clearly, pointing to the man's side.

"Your counterpart is, even now, hidden *in* you!" declared the Lord. "Counterpart shall be not only *for* you, but *of* you and *by* you–of your life, of your substance. Counterpart will be *your* being. She shall be you, extended! Bone of your bone. Flesh of your flesh. Being of your being. Essence of your essence."

"Oh!" exclaimed one of the angels quietly as he tilted slightly to whisper to another. "Then it is not creation at all. It is a building matter, of sorts."

"But what of God's oneness?" asked a still-curious angel.

"How should I know?" came the befuddled reply. "We have been here only since the foundation of the ages and the beginning of time and eternity . . . not *before*!"

The whispering faded. The Lord was staring at man. Slowly he raised his hand and passed it over the face of man.

Again the angels gasped.

Man slipped to the ground and lay very still. Indeed, *too* still.

"Has the inward portion . . . ceased to exist?"

"I believe not, he still glows."

"But how can *anything* be so . . . so still?"

"Let us trust, even in this strange sight, that all things in God's creation are still good."

Now if one thrusts his hand into water, he shall surely bring forth water. And, perchance, if one thrusts his hand into the earth, he shall surely bring forth earth. It follows, then, that should the Living God thrust his hand into the side of man, he would surely bring forth humanity. And this very thing he did, drawing forth from *within* man a portion of that man. A part of the man's own being was now *separated* from man, yet that portion was still of man.

Angels stood dumbstruck, watching man cease to be one, and yet remaining one.

"You see," said the Lord softly, "there is something . . . *someone* . . . hidden *in* Adam."

The Lord brought forth from man's side a bone–a softly *glowing* bone–and held it up for all to see.

"The man is no longer one. He is divided, yet both parts are . . . still that man," declared the Lord.

"Never could I have conceived that such a thing could be," spoke one of the angels to himself. "Truly, there are many wonders to be found in the ways of God."

The Lord God now turned to face the angelic host.

"From this bone, taken from the inward parts of man, I shall *build* his mate."

"He . . ." The Lord's voice trembled. Every angel tensed, a few instinctively reaching for their swords.

"Man . . . shall now have one beside him. One of his very substance, his being . . . extended. I shall now build flesh from his flesh. Bone from his bone. Thus shall he gain a counterpart. A counterpart who is oneness. A counterpart upon whom he may pour out . . . his love."

As one, the angels bowed their faces to the earth. Some small revelation of the unfolding drama had made its way into their spirits. They stood again and began to sing softly as Creator now became Builder.

Soon the singing gave way to silence, for the scene before them enthralled their whole being.

CHAPTER 5

"BEHOLD, NO INCONSISTENCY IS HERE," said one of the angels, resuming his quiet inquiry. "In our realm, in the *invisibles*, there are no counterparts. But here in man's realm–in the visible world–*all* things have counterparts. So, it is a natural thing for man also to have a counterpart." The angel rose to his full height, as one about to bring to conclusion a great mystery. "It is a matter of visible or *not* visible. Though man is the image of God, he *is* visible. And God is invisible. Therein lies the difference! Invisible, spiritual . . . no mate. Visible, physical . . . a mate."

"Still," wondered the audience of one that stood beside him, "still, if the *image* can have a mate, why then cannot God thc *original*–have a mate? And besides, man is not *just* of the physical realm. He is partly of the spiritual. He is not wholly like the animals, you know. He glows!"

The whispered conversation ended abruptly.

As the Lord worked, the form of the new being was becoming

discernible. Suddenly one of the archangels–the angel of light–moved through the throng and approached the Lord. A murmur of astonishment rose from the heavenly host. That anyone would intrude upon their Lord at such a moment was quite . . . unangelic!

"Might I form in words what each of us has asked within our spirits?"

"You may," replied the Lord.

"You are fashioning for man a counterpart. Will you also create for *yourself* a counterpart?"

Consternation broke out in angelic ranks. Never had such conduct been seen, nor a question so inappropriate been conceived. And, surely, *never* had such a question ever been asked.

The Lord's answer came unnervingly calm.

"Creation is ended. How can I create, when creation is over? No, by the immutability of my own nature, and the sureness of my word, the matter of creating is forever ended."

There was a finality in this declaration that ended all questions.

The archangel relaxed, but all the other angels tensed.

"No," came the Lord's voice, again so calm, so quiet that angels strained to hear. "Neither man nor . . . I . . ." He paused. "Neither man, nor any other, shall have a counterpart from out of this creation. *Creating* has ended. Furthermore, you may mark this hour the last counterpart *this* creation will ever see."

He now turned to address the archangel face to face. "It would necessitate a whole new creation, and therefore the end of this one, to perform so grand a deed. Nor could *I* ever have a *created* counterpart. Kind after my kind would, necessarily, have to be *uncreated*–would it not–for *I* am uncreated! Nonetheless . . ."

The conversation ended. The Lord returned to his work. The archangel, his curiosity somewhat assuaged, returned to his appointed place above the angels, and beside the throne.

Now, more intently than ever, the Builder returned to fashioning the shimmering, glowing form that had been, only moments before, but the rib of a man. Quite abruptly and unexpectedly, he stopped.

So perfect was his stillness it chilled the heavenly host. Slowly, at first imperceptibly, the light within the Lord began to brighten. And it grew brighter yet as revelation within him intensified. Angelic alarm broke out as this growing light began to envelop first the angels, then the earth, then the galaxy. Upward, outward the light soared until its brightness had swallowed up all visible creation.

There was no question. Not since the moment when God first conceived of creating had the brightness of revelation known such brilliance.

Still higher–and brighter–the light ascended, pouring into the heavenly places, filling every crevice of the invisible realms. The length and breadth of creation was now swallowed up in the glory of the light of God as he considered this matter of . . . a counterpart!

The angels crumbled in terror before such brightness. Their own spirits, now immersed in God, began to touch the thought of God. They were drowning in bursts of spiraling revelation.

Slowly the revelation subsided, giving angels a moment to wonder what *ultimate* thought had coursed through God's being. What masterpiece might now fall from his hand? At last they could pierce the light and see again the face of God. Upon that face was etched exaltation and joy.

Whispered one angel as he staggered to his appointed place, "He has contemplated man's counterpart. He has *seen* her in the eye of his mind. But somewhere beyond that sight, methinks, he has glimpsed a higher, far greater revelation. But what?"

"'Tis mystery, hidden in unapproachable light," rejoined another.

Now it was with trembling hands that the Builder did build, and mold, and fashion, and mold again. And while the being he fashioned took on its final form, awed and dumbfounded angels fell once more to their knees at the sight of the wonder before them.

One angel, most irreverently, cried aloud the thoughts of all: "He is not making another Ish. This one is alike, yet different. As the lioness is to the lion, so is this *out-of-man.* But never, never," cried the wayward angel, "was lion or lioness so beautiful as this."

Another angel broke the confines of restraint.

"Nor was even man so beautiful as this!" he exclaimed.

With that, the vaults of heaven broke open, and in one full-throated shout, all heavenly beings proclaimed:

Never was
nor e'er shall be
as beautiful
a thing as she.
All hosts in
heaven's court,
all creatures on
earthen sod,
it matters not
the tribe nor race,
one sight alone can
be
more beautiful than
she.
It is the face
of God.

CHAPTER 6

"I AM SURE I UNDERSTAND IT NOW."

"And what is that?"

"The light . . . the light that a moment ago almost consumed us! Our God cannot have a counterpart; nonetheless, he saw within his eye what she might be . . . *if* ever she could exist . . . *the counterpart of God.* By revelation he saw what she would be if he had an Ishah! Then he held that vision before him, a vision of *his own mate . . .* and then fashioned the bone of man into a counterpart. Do you not realize? This *she* is fashioned in the image of his vision of his own counterpart! The mate of man is a picture of that counterpart of God, which God will never have."

"If this one formed by the hand of God is an image, ah, then what might God's counterpart be, if indced she could be?"

"'Tis a thing we shall never know."

"Nor shall our God."

"It is no wonder then," continued the angel, "that having completed this supreme masterpiece–as I am sure you noted–our Lord knows but a melancholy joy."

CHAPTER 7

THE LORD STEPPED BACK from the pulsating form that all might see her. A living, breathing creature lay quietly at his feet, robed in an iridescent glow. She appeared as one who might have been chiseled out of sunlight.

For a long moment the angels gazed at this wholly new being whose form, contour, and features were beyond all imagination to conceive or mind to capture.

Here was a counterpart to man, kind after his kind. And now–all knew–there could be sons of man and daughters of man . . . after *his* kind.

Man–the image of God–having "after his kind" was a thought that had never before crossed their spirits.

It was *out-of-man* who broke the angelic spell. She opened her eyes and looked curiously about. As she rose, a cry of delight issued from the angels as they beheld such regal grace. At last her eyes fell upon the face of God. She tilted her head slightly, as curiosity gave way to wisdom.

"Thou art my Lord, my Creator and my God."

"I am," came the Lord's soft reply.

She cast her eyes far across the celestial host, then turned again to her Lord.

"There is but *one* of you," she observed.

Then, smiling, she gestured toward the angels.

"There are *many* of you.

"And I . . . am I but one? Or am I many?"

The answer came as quickly as it came surprisingly, for it came in but one word.

"Go," said the Lord, pointing in a direction quite opposite from where the man lay sleeping.

"Go. Beyond the angels. Beyond the animals. To the hills. To the mountains. Go, and there await."

The woman stretched out her hand and touched the hand of God, then turned and disappeared into the west.

The Lord turned and moved toward the east. The angels followed, their thoughts all one.

"She was in man. She was hidden right there, in him! Unseen, unconceived of . . . by any mortal mind. Yet there she was, all the time, *in* him. She was an unrevealed mystery hidden *in* man.

"And the Ancient of Days, we know him well, yet not at all.

"Long before we came, what other mystery might there have been?

"What thing, what glorious *mystery* might yet be hidden *in* him?

"A counterpart *in* God? Kind after his kind? Being of his being? Nature of his nature? And . . . sons of God! And daughters of God!

"Could it be that hidden in God is a . . . No! Of course not. The thought is unthinkable!"

CHAPTER 8

THE LORD GAZED INTENTLY at the opening in man's side. Time seemed to move forward before his eyes. He was looking upon some distant scene no other eyes could see. Sadness fell across his face as he knelt down before the quiet, still form of the man.

"So this is the way it is . . . and shall be," he said, almost in a moan. Tenderly he closed the wound–the wound from whence had come *man's* counterpart.

The Lord then whispered to the motionless form before him. "Once you were one, yet a great mystery was in you. Now you are two. But as is my nature, so is yours. You must soon be *one . . . again*!"

Man opened his eyes, and with the first instant of consciousness he frantically grabbed his side. His eyes widened.

"Hallelujah!" he exclaimed. "Something is missing!"

He sprang to his feet and whirled about, exclaiming, "Where is she! Where is my out-of-man?"

"Man," responded a calm but much ignored Lord, "I would walk with you for a moment."

"Yes! Yes! But where is she?"

The Lord waited.

Man dropped his hands, turned toward the Lord, and smiled. "You have made angels swift, yet your ways are sometimes slower even than mine!" With that he joined his Lord, and together they walked.

"Your substance has been divided, man. Yet it remains the same. She is of you, out of you, from you, and one with you . . . yet now separate.

"You are, and ever shall be, my image. Therefore she must return to you, this substance of your substance. She must become, once more, *one* with *you.*"

"I do not fully understand all that you have said," replied the man slowly.

"It is not necessary that you understand. But it is important that you pour out your love on her. For now, at last, your love has somewhere to go."

Betraying some hidden doubt, man responded, "I have never expressed this love that beats within me. Will I . . ."

"I have fashioned from your being a *she.* And, yes, you will know how to express that love that is now still captured within you."

"And . . . and then?"

"Counterpart will, of course, return that love to you."

The man stopped. "You mean," he responded, stunned at the idea now coursing through him, "you mean that love shall not only be given, but shall also be *received*? Love will be returned?"

The Lord's own being trembled at the word. "Yes. Given . . . *and* received," he replied.

Turning to fix his full gaze upon the face of God, the man inquired, "And what shall such an experience be likened to, to receive love from *an other than* . . . to receive love from a counterpart?"

A deep look of sadness crossed over that incomparable face.

"There resides in the council of my being an exchange of fellowship . . . and of love about which you know nothing. *Within* my being courses a love of Fatherhood and Sonhood . . . of which you are but a reflection. The depth and breadth of *this* love is beyond all mortal conception. But the love of a counterpart . . . this is a matter of discovery you will know and I shall never. . . . It is a matter you will know *before* I know!

"Now, wait here. Wait, until you see . . . or hear."

With those words the Lord disappeared.

CHAPTER 9

TO FILL THE VACANCY OF HER SOLITUDE, she had wandered deep into unexplored places, pausing now and again to admire the handiwork of her Lord's creation. The ocean of aloneness that surrounded her, nonetheless, began to engulf her whole being.

An outward cry of despair, to give expression to some inward longing, was about to rise from her throat when the Lord suddenly appeared before her. For a long moment he studied the deep loneliness so evident upon her face.

"Is there something here in my creation that is not good?" inquired the Lord.

"My Lord, my God, my Creator, this creation is beautiful beyond all explaining. But I am here, all alone."

"Yes, I know. I, too, have dwelt in aloneness for a very long time."

"Shall I ever be alone? Am I the only one of my kind?"

"I shall answer that question now," replied the Lord. "I will summon all earthly creatures to this place."

With that, he raised his hand. Far away, all animals of all kinds turned to face the west.

As the multitude of beasts swarmed across the horizon, they gradually formed a vast circle around their Lord and the beautiful creature beside him.

"Always they come by two," she observed quietly.

"Gaze carefully upon them, Eve, and as you do, listen to the spirit within you."

Instantly Eve sensed, for the first time, a place within her . . . some deep, hidden, *spiritual* place. And with that discovery she laid hold of a whole new realm of her being. Revelation burned within her.

Now the revelation gave way to utterance.

"All things here are in their proper order. Yet something of my life is *not* in order."

As the last animal passed before her, she again faced her Creator, yet no word was uttered.

The Lord raised his hand and pointed toward a distant place, and with that the two began the ascent of a very high mountain.

"I am beautiful," said Eve at last, speaking in a childlike innocence. "Perhaps more beautiful than any of the other creatures. Thou hast made me so. And I can love. No . . . I *do* love. But there is none to love."

She stopped abruptly.

"I am a lioness, yet there is no lion."

With a faint note of joy slipping into his words, the Lord responded, "Truly, you are an incredible creature." Then smiling softly, he added, "And, yes, I have made you so! You are perfect, Eve. As perfect as anything *created* can be perfect. Nor can you–or any other creature–reach beyond your present perfection, except you take into yourself that which is *not created.*"

"I understand not, my Lord."

"It is *divinity* alone that is *truly* perfect," he replied.

"But you have not answered my question, Eve. Is there anything in my creation that is not good?"

The woman paused, struggling with the question, seeking to form an answer. Suddenly a smile broke across her face.

"But, my Lord, I cannot answer your question until you have answered mine. Am I alone, or is there another like unto me?"

"What joyful company you will make for your mate . . . if such a mate exists!" replied the Lord with a delighted laugh.

"Does one?" she queried again.

"Eve, you are not alone. Yes, there is one like you. And . . . Eve . . . he waits, even now, for you.

"Go! Go, and find him."

With those words the Lord once again disappeared.

And Eve whispered, "Then, my Lord, I will answer your question. Yes! All things *are* good."

CHAPTER 10

SHE MOVED IN AN EVER-WIDENING CIRCLE, sometimes traversing meadows, sometimes climbing hills, but always searching. The intense longing within her heart grew with every passing hour. But always, there was no *he* to be found.

In desperation she stretched her hands toward the heavens and cried, "Where is he? Where is my *he*?"

She heard again the words of her God: "Listen to the spirit, deep within you."

With that, the spirit within her leaped. The soft glow that covered her shown now in almost angelic intensity. She sensed the air, and there, on the highest of mountains, called forth the ends of her strength to cry aloud.

"Lord! Lord Adam! Come! Come, Lord Adam. Come quickly!"

Once more she sensed the air about her. Once more the glow of her spirit leaped outward in renewed brightness. Whirling about toward the east, she began running with all her might.

CHAPTER 11

FAR BEYOND THE DISTANT HORIZON, upon another mountain, a weary and saddened man shot to his feet, turning westward as he did. Something within his spirit had leaped. He glowed now with a light that surely matched any angel's.

"She is there. Somewhere. I sense her. She is calling. For *me*!"

Consumed with excitement, he plunged down the mountain, leaping streams, circumventing boulders, and vaulting rills. There was near madness in his westward plunge.

He was certain now. She was near, and she, too, was moving . . . toward him . . . and with the same abandon.

Never before, never since, has a man moved so swiftly. The very air whistled in his path.

Across plain and meadow she came, hesitating only long enough to sense again the deep instincts of her spiritual being. Then she bolted forth again to press the laws of nature in her speed.

Unknown to either, their paths would meet at the very entrance to the Garden of Eden.

For one bright instant, though still far away, he glimpsed her. "I saw her. She is out there. I saw her! A lighted figure, like unto me. I saw her, but she has disappeared." Once more he lunged into flight.

Then, in a far-distant place, this time not with spirit but with ear, he heard, "Come, Lord Adam, come!"

Half mad he leaped toward the echo of the sound, fairly screaming:

Behold, I come! I come!

Out from behind one of the vast roots of the Tree of Life, the glowing figure appeared again! He could see her clearly now, more beautiful than anything his imagination had ever conceived. She disappeared again from view, leaving the man quite at the end of sanity.

"My she, my she!" he cried, half running, half stumbling. Surely she had seen him, he thought. "And she matched me in flight. She desires to come to *me*!" With that he found himself not only running and weeping, but thundering,

I love you. I love you. Do you hear? I love you!

She came once more into view. The space separating them was closing fast. Each halted very suddenly, not at all sure what next to do. Then man roared again, "Do you hear? I love you!" Spontaneously, they flew into one another's arms as he heard her unequivocal reply. "I love you, too. I love you . . . as you love me."

With joy, with shouts, with laughter, and with tears, they clung to one another in wild embrace, yet all the while the man continued to cry, "You are beautiful. More beautiful than archangels. And I love you, I love you."

As she could, she replied, "And I love you, too."

Laughing in quiet delirium and exulting in uninhibited joy, he released his embrace and held her high in his mighty arms. He threw back his head and bellowed to the heavens,

I love!
At last, I love.
And love has been returned.

With the excitement of a child, he held her at arm's length and cried again, quite beside himself, "Did you know? Did you know that you were once in *me*? Hidden *in* me! Here. See! You! Such a beautiful creature as you. *In me.* Right here in my side. That is where you were. And did you know–you are made . . . of *me*! We . . . were . . . separated. Now look at us. We are together again. You have returned to me!" He pulled her toward him, whirling about as he did.

"Together. Forever!"

His final words seemed to roll across creation.

Now holding her beside himself, he glanced quickly around, then raised his hand toward the heavens.

Creator, Lord.
Hear me!
Angels, hear me!
Seraphim and cherubim.
Creatures of the deep,
upon the land,
and in the sky.
I am one once more.
Behold, my counterpart!
More beautiful, more glorious
than all realms combined.
At last!

Bone of my bone,
flesh of my flesh.
And I . . . man!
Your earthen lord . . . I . . .
I . . . am . . . no . . . longer . . . alone!
Hear me,
realms seen.
Hear me,
realms unseen.
The aloneness is broken
forever!
And now, my Lord,
my God,
my Creator–
It was not good for
Man
to be alone.
And I am not alone.
Henceforth,
forever,
All things are good.

"There remains but one thing, the ultimate completion of all oneness–first . . . *you* in me, now . . . *I . . . in you!*"

So it came about, there in the serene beauty of the Garden of Eden, a place more beautiful than heaven and earth, he embraced her again. And while angels rejoiced in that primordial age of innocence, the ruler of earth and his counterpart became, once more . . . one flesh.

CHAPTER 12

UNNOTICED BY ANY CREATED EYE, the Lord God quietly withdrew. While angels broke forth in exultation at man's joy, the Lord rose above the earth, above the sky. He returned to heavenly realms, and yet again he ascended. Above and beyond even heavenly realms, he rose. Back to that nonplace, outside time, outside eternity . . . back to where he was the *All.*

There, utterly alone, as alone he had so long been, the Lord God released from the depths of his heart a cry of sorrow.

No. No!
Man!
*All things are **not** good.*
It is not good
that God
should be alone!

CHAPTER 13

THERE ARE ANGELS MORE CURIOUS than others, and the afternoon of the eighth day found two of the more curious musing over the events of the morning.

"There is much I do not fully comprehend."

"Such as. . . ?"

"The woman was *in* the man. True?"

"As we both bore witness!"

"And man is the image of God, is he not? Then is there something that is even now *in* God?"

"You are asking me?"

"I am. And I am asking you yet another matter. Man and his counterpart, were they not united again–once more utterly *one*? And was it not true that there, in the garden, he was *in* her?"

"So it was."

"And man is the physical and visible image of an invisible God! Is he not a physical *picture* of spiritual reality?"

"You have already asked that question once," replied the other.

"Well, to the point. Is it not possible that one day, in the realms of the *spirituals*, the Lord God might also be *in* something . . . or someone . . . who was first hidden *in* him. That one, in him. He, in that one?"

"I suppose, *if* there is someone now hidden in God, then it might follow that one day God shall be hidden in that someone! Perhaps. I do not know. I am, after all, only an immortal angel."

CHAPTER 14

THE LORD EXTENDED AN INVITATION to the man and woman to make their abode in Eden, the very Paradise of God.

Often they walked with him there, and as they did, they spoke with him of many things. But on occasion he withdrew–that is, from *their* view. In a distant place he would watch–and consider the ways of this living image of himself.

"They are never distracted from one another, for there is no distraction. In their eyes, nothing else exists!

"She has no blemish; she has no wrinkle. There is nothing imperfect in all her being.

"He loves her continuously. And with abandoned, innocent, unbridled passion, she loves him in return.

"She has full confidence in her place beside him. No reassurances need be given that he loves her. She never questions, but totally accepts his love. There is no fear of displeasing him or losing him.

"She is beautiful, she knows that, yet there is no pride. Rather, a deep inward knowing that he is lord of all earth, and she is . . . his perfect mate."

The Lord God turned and moved away. But not before he smiled and whispered to himself:

And when that wondrous
day arrives, so shall these
things be true . . . of my Eve.

PART 2

CHAPTER 15

HE HAD STOOD THERE ALL MORNING, high upon the summit of a great desert mountain, watching intently toward the south. Finally, in late afternoon, it began to appear, first as a tiny speck on the horizon, gradually growing until it became a moving sea of humanity. It was his people, lately set free from slavery.

Tomorrow, he knew, he would meet with their leader on this very mount and speak to him face to face of many things that weighed upon his heart.

For a moment, though, his thoughts wandered back to the Garden of Eden, to the disobedience, to the horrible fall of man and the fall of all creation. He recalled again the Flood and Noah. The water had hardly receded when the cycle of failure had commenced yet again.

Today he would begin once more. And what would be the outcome?

The fleeing refugees were coming into clear focus now. He could make out Moses in the lead, the mohair tents, the cattle and sheep, even the vague outline of his people. He stared at this moving mass of humanity until the image before him blurred and began to change in form and, finally, became but one person. His eyes now saw not a multitude of people, but only a lovely young girl, coming up from Egypt, crossing the hot sands and moving toward him.

"She will be here by evening. Soon she will enter the land I have promised to her. There she will reach full womanhood. I have waited since before eternity. I have created the whole reaches of the cosmos for but this one Purpose.

"I wonder . . . I wonder. Will she learn to love me?"

CHAPTER 16

THOUGH HE WAS WELL OVER EIGHTY NOW, the man moved with a quick and sure foot as he mounted a huge rock around which a million people were gathered. They had come, on this grand occasion, to hear him speak. Slowly, but in a loud, clear voice, he began to recount to them the tale of their long and venerable history, bringing again to their minds the miraculous events of the last few days.

"After the great Flood, when all mankind was destroyed because of their wickedness and because they had forgotten their God, the family of Noah again brought forth children. Once more the race of man covered the earth, and once again the sons of man turned from their God and filled the earth with their iniquity.

"For the second time the Lord God repented that he had made man. He gave them up. Once more he called forth a single family to follow him. Today, all about you, you see the descendants of that family. A nation has come forth from Abraham, Isaac, and Jacob.

"Today the Lord God has called this people to return to the land where once dwelt our ancestor Abraham. Upon that land, and from that land, we are destined to live.

"It is to *you* that the Lord has turned his great love. But be not proud. For it is not that you are a fair and noble people that he loves you. No! For you are the sons and daughters of slaves, a people despised. Nor is it because you are a great and large nation that he loves you. No! For you are the smallest of all nations.

"Then why does he love you?

"He loves you . . . because he loves you.

"Today we journey once again toward that land that the Lord gave to our father, Abraham. When you have entered that land, you will grow strong and prosper. In *that* day, do not forget your God. Turn not to the ways of the nations surrounding you. Fill that land with iniquity as other nations fill theirs, and you will surely learn the Lord's displeasure. Even his wrath.

"Remember his mercy to us, his faithfulness in the land of Egypt and beside the sea. Had it not been for his mercy, that sea would surely, even now, be our grave.

"And what is it the Lord asks of you . . . this day . . . and in the day you enter the land he has promised to you?

"I have stood before him, face to face. I have seen his holiness . . . yet lived! I have watched his power . . . unlimited. I have drowned in his glory . . . indescribable.What does such a God require of us? But one thing. Above all else, *one* thing." Moses paused, then cried out,

Love him
With all your might.
Love him
With all your mind.
Love him
With all your soul.
Love him
With all your being.
Love him!

CHAPTER 17

AS THE GREAT THRONG BROKE UP, the words of Moses still ringing in ears and hearts, the people returned thoughtfully to their tents. And as they gathered in those dwellings, they shared their hearts.

Among one family, of the tribe of Levi, there occurred this conversation.

"Oh, father, I do love him. I wish to serve him. This very day I shall speak with Aaron. I wish to devote my whole life to serving our wondrous Lord . . . his dwelling . . . and his people."

A short distance away, a wife turned to her husband, searched his face for a moment, and then spoke her heart.

"Oh, husband. In Egypt ours was a lot far easier than most of our countrymen. And the gifts given us upon our departure were no small things, for either slave or free. I see in your eyes that your thoughts are mine. Our God is so gracious, so kind, and we do love him, with all our hearts. All that we have of silver and gold, let us give to him."

Quick and eager was the husband's response. "Yes, with a heart of love, let us give him such as we have."

And in another tribe, far distant from the Levites, a group of fervent young men spoke in grave and measured words.

"It is agreed. Today, here and now, we make a solemn vow to our Lord and to one another. We will forever obey the voice of our God. What he speaks we will do. Always. Whatever he asks, be it a small thing or be it our very lives, we will obey the voice of the Lord. If he speaks in the silent places of our hearts or in the hearing of our ears, or be it to Moses that he should speak, his demand shall instantly be our will, as long as breath is in us."

"'Tis not enough," broke in another. "Prayer! Let us covenant to pray. To be men of prayer, upon our knees, seeking his face, allowing him to search our hearts. Yes, and asking for power to do his will in hours of need and crisis."

As they spoke of these things, an elder of the tribe rushed by, hurriedly seeking out the other leaders of his tribe. Having found them, he spoke in fervent terms.

"This we must do! Tomorrow let our tribe assemble. Let us come with our cymbals and trumpets. Behold–here in my hand–already a song has been written by one of our youth. 'Tis a psalm exhorting us to extol the ways of our God. Let us take this song and other psalms of praise; let us render them unto our Lord and fall down upon our faces and worship him together."

Eagerly the elders agreed, "Surely there is no better way to show our love for our God than to pour out our worship before him."

By nightfall the great rock upon which Moses had spoken was vacant, except for one lone figure. Unobserved by all, he had been there listening–listening to Moses recount to the people his very own message to them. Afterward he had walked among his people, listening intently to their every word.

A deep sadness now disturbed the face of the Lord, for he was contemplating the response he had heard from his people.

A long, deep groan of sorrow, unheard by human ears but

shattering the tranquility of the entire heavenly host, rose up from his depths.

I did not require of you
your wealth nor coins of gold.
What need have I of these?
I did not ask of you
that you serve me.
Do I, the Mighty One,
need to be waited upon?
Neither did I ask of you
your worship nor your prayers
nor even your obedience.

He paused. Once more a long, mournful groan rose from his breast.

I have asked but this of you,
that you love me . . .
love me . . .
love me.

CHAPTER 18

IN THE EYES OF EARTHEN MAN she was a nation, but through the eyes of God she was a woman. A nation, yes, but in his sight a composite woman who foreshadowed his bride. He also knew what no angel nor man knew–nor even dreamed: Out from her would one day come his bride. Therefore he loved this one, visited her, counseled her.

There were those who vied for her love and who sought to embrace her. There were also those who would destroy her. The Lord God watched carefully such suitors *and* enemies. He remembered his rivals, he marked her enemies, he noted *her* weaknesses and chronicled her every distraction and distracter.

Recalling a serpent that had once beguiled Eve, he vowed, "*That one* must go!" Recalling that a simple thing like bread had caused her to stumble in the wilderness, he affirmed within his being, "When there comes the daughter of this woman, that daughter shall not live by bread alone."

He saw the world and its glittery trinkets distract her, and he swore by himself, "That glitter, and its author, will I annihilate." But most of all, he observed the utter weakness and helplessness of her life in the face of any temptation and all sin. Once more he was provoked to declare, "Her daughter–my bride–shall live, by *another* and higher life!"

CHAPTER 19

OUT OF EGYPT HAD COME THIS GIRL. She crossed a searing wilderness, and in the land of promise she found rest and prosperity. But in her prosperity she moved farther and farther from her Lord.

Again and again he issued forth to her a cry:

Return to me.
Return to me!

But return she would not. Rather she went awhoring with the nations of the world.

Unnoticed by her, but well observed by her enemies, her wayward wandering from her God had caused her to lose the great strength he had bestowed upon her.

At last a brokenhearted God was forced to cry,
Do you not know I love you?

Yet though I love you
I must chasten you.
And when you wander from me,
there is no higher proof of my love
than this:
I will chastise you
and thereby bring you back to myself.

So she fell from weakness to weakness. A nation once abundant in strength and greatness became the vassal of even the weakest of nations.

Still she would not return to him.

"There is left to me, then, no other resource but one," sighed the Lord.

CHAPTER 20

HE BEGAN TO CALL FORTH PROPHETS—men born in the South–to go into all the land to warn his people of coming judgment.

The prophets went forth, crying out again and again,

Repent!
Repent!
Turn back to the Lord,
your lover.

Some of these prophets journeyed to the North and cried out against the wantonness and godlessness of the people there.

To these prophets the people of the South listened only slightly; the North listened not at all.

There were no prophets from the North. There was, though, a young man from the North who fell in love with a most beautiful young girl in his village. He poured out upon her his whole affection, and soon they were married. But just as soon, she left him–to sell her body for the pleasures of sin. She made her abode in the world; and in its dregs and in her wickedness, she forgot the young man who had loved her so.

It was to the ears of this young man that there came, one awful day, the voice of the Lord.

Go, Hosea, go to your people.
Cry out to them.
Cry out with tongue,
cry out with pen.
Denounce their
evil deeds.
Call them to me.

But before you go,
search through this land.
Find that woman
of harlotry;
bring her to your
home.
Make her, once more,
your bride.

Hosea clutched his ears at hearing these words. In revulsion he wept at the thought of touching again one so unclean. Nonetheless, he obeyed. From village to village he sought her. In dark and foul places he searched until at last he found her–found her in stupefying sin and filthy indifference.

Into his arms he lifted her, brought her into his home, and betrothed her again to himself.

"What have you done, Hosea?" came the voice of the Lord.

"Though she be a whore, I have taken her back," replied Hosea.

"So . . . I . . . the Lord God, will also receive again this whore, Israel. I will search her out in her sin; I will forgive her and bring her again into my house."

And together they sat down, and together they wept.

CHAPTER 21

WHEN THE CUP WAS FULL and the time complete, the Lord allowed the North to be swept forever from the pages of history. And when grace had reached its ends, the Lord allowed the South to be conquered and the whole people led off in chains, across hot, dreary, and endless deserts, to another land.

Days turned to weeks as they traversed those burning sands. With each step they dragged their chains and thought of their forefathers in Egypt. At last they came to a city that once worshiped God but now worshiped bugs. A people whom God had once led out of slavery was led into slavery by that same Lord.

CHAPTER 22

BEHOLD ONE, THERE, trudging along a hot dusty road in southern Babylon. For twenty-two years he has made his weary way from village to village, from city to city, comforting God's people, assuring them of eventual deliverance, and rebuking them for their sin. His shoulders are bent, his body stooped, for he carries in his soul the burden of his home, even the city of God, lying far away . . . still and desolate, a heap of ashes. His heart is filled, even at this moment, with sad and youthful memories of her destruction . . . and of a people who would not turn again to their Lord.

As the old man fought his way against hot winds and blowing sands of this Chaldean wasteland, his solitary thoughts were invaded by a small, shrill cry. The old prophet whirled about to discover the source of so tiny and so pitiable a call. Running to the side of the road, he furiously pulled back the dried bushes, there to discover, lying in the ditch, a newborn babe. Its body was wrapped in the sack of afterbirth, its cord uncut. The child was gasping its last, small breath.

The old prophet ripped open the sack and breathed into the infant's lungs. Clutching the filthy child to his bosom, he ran toward the nearest house.

Late that evening the weary old man bade good night to a childless family among his own people who had taken the infant. As he slipped out onto the dusty road once more, his mind remained transfixed on the tragic state of the child whose life he had saved. A stirring was beginning to evidence itself deep in his heart when he heard a voice from behind him.

Ezekiel!

The old prophet stopped. He dared not move nor even breathe, for he knew too well that voice. And its coming did not always bode well for him.

Ezekiel!

"Yes, my Lord," he replied to open skies.

"The child . . . the one you found in the ditch."

"Yes, Lord."

"Ezekiel, as you did, I once walked down a desolate road. I, too, heard the cry of a tiny infant. It, too, was wrapped in its mother's afterbirth, and it, too, was dying. The mother of that dying babe was a Hittite, unclean. Its father, an Amorite, unclean! The child was an ugly, unloved, unlovable, filthy outcast . . . born of uncleanliness.

"I grasped that child to my bosom. I brought it to my home; there I washed the child, rubbed it with salt, nurtured and cared for it.

"The child was a girl. I gave her a name, *Jeru.* And because *I* raised her, she grew to be strong and beautiful. She was among the most beautiful of all women. In the days of Solomon she had become the most beautiful woman upon the face of the earth."

There was a long, dreadful pause. Ezekiel shuddered.

"On the day I would have taken her for my bride–on *that* day she heard the call of Egypt and Babylon. To them she gave up her virginity and her purity. She turned from me, walked the ways of the world, gave herself to fallen love. She became a harlot to Egypt and a slave in Babylon.

"Her gold they took from her; her silver, too. In the place of freedom, bondage. Instead of beauty, wrinkles. Her loveliness earned her only ruin. Yet, even now–though enslaved–Jeru will not return to me.

"Ezekiel, do you know of what I speak?"

Ezekiel turned his worn old face to the heavens, clamped his eyes closed, and in tight, measured words, responded. "Oh, my God, I know. I know!"

"For *me*, Ezekiel, go to that woman. Prophesy to her. Tell her to return to me. I will give her salve for her sores, clean garments for her rags. I will restore to her the beauty of her youth if she will but turn again to me."

There was another pause. Ezekiel's face turned again, his heart ached within his breast as he awaited once more the voice of the Lord. When it came, it came with such pathos that Ezekiel clutched his hands to his ears, trying to hold back the sound of the agonizing of God.

Return to me, Jeru.
Return to your Creator.

I have asked nothing
save this,
that you love me.

With your mind,
your heart,
your soul,
love me!

Jeru, Jeru,
return to me.
Turn from your harlotry.
Turn back,
O city,
turn back.
Turn back, O bride of God.

Return to me,
O Jerusalem!

CHAPTER 23

AS THE YEARS ROLLED ON, the story of the wayward nation changed but little. The beautiful woman strayed . . . returned . . . and strayed again. Each time she strayed, the Lord marked well those things that enticed her from him.

Patiently he watched the centuries come and go, waiting for the time he would step through the Door that separated time from eternity and there, on the stage of human drama, play out the role of the central figure of history.

And when he had marked every weakness and every enemy, he whispered, "The fullness of time is come. I am through with images, foreshadowings, symbols, and pictures! Now shall come reality. Now I shall have my counterpart."

He stepped from his throne and whispered to himself, "There is a village in Galilee." He raised his hand and called to one of the archangels.

Gabriel!

CHAPTER 24

TO THAT ENIGMATIC PLACE, the portal between the physical and spiritual realms, he came. He had approached this Door many times before, had stepped out of the spiritual realm and plunged into the physical world, there to visit briefly for the purpose of some declaration, to alter history's spastic course, or to speak face to face with one of his prophets.

Today though, angels noted, something was different. As he stood before the open Door, rage burned upon his face; his eyes glowed white hot. In all their long acquaintance with him they had never beheld such anger. Suddenly, a cry of terror ascended from the angels.

The Lord God *had disappeared.*

No more than an instant passed before they *knew* what he had done. And still amazement grew.

Often they had wondered why there remained but one who had

no mate. Yet surely he would take no bride from angels nor fallen man. Nor could he–against his own word–create again.

He was a God of mystery, and somehow they *knew* his vanishing had something to do with a counterpart.

In that moment of consternation, Gabriel lifted his hand and announced:

Universal history is about to know
its greatest hour.
The Lord God is about to
incarnate himself
in the womb
of woman
and come forth
in the form
of human flesh.

Silence reigned for a moment. Grasping Gabriel's words and their meaning was beyond the bounds of angelic understanding.

What was it, there inside their God, that would drive him to such ends? God . . . in a likeness of fallen human flesh? A human in the form of a roach was more plausible.

Why? was their unspoken query.

"A counterpart," was their agreement.

"How?" was their unanimous question.

"We do not know," was their final conclusion.

His bride from the fallen human race, like Hosea's? Is it possible? The Holy God? Perhaps he will somehow seek to redeem her; but nothing that fallen could ever be *that* redeemed.

And yet, there it was: If he truly were to be born of a woman he would be God . . . visible. And if he were to become one of earth's inhabitants, he would be living in the realm where *all* species have a counterpart.

Obviously, there was something he knew that they did not know, a dimension of truth sealed off from their understanding.

This dimension of angelic ignorance became even more evident when they discovered he had chosen for his place of earthly birth not a castle, but a barn.

PART 3

CHAPTER 25

THE LITTLE BOY THRUST HIS HEAD THROUGH the partially open door and stared at the perspiring young man busy mending a piece of broken furniture.

"Have you heard the desert prophet?" inquired the little boy.

"No," came the genial reply of the young carpenter. "I have been quite occupied here of late. I am working alone now, as you know."

"Yes, and we all miss Joseph very much," came the little boy's quiet and sad response. "But anyway, I'm going to hear the desert prophet. Will you?"

"Yes," replied the carpenter, laying aside his finished work. "It is time I visited this prophet causing such a stir out there."

"Perhaps I will meet you there," replied the little boy. The door began to close, then opened again suddenly. The little boy's head reappeared.

"Is he not your brother, or something?"

"He is my cousin," came the reply.

"Ohhh, you must be very proud!" was the awed response.

"Very," replied the carpenter. "Very, very proud."

The door closed. The young carpenter looked about the room slowly, then–hesitantly–stored his mallet, his chisel, his tools of carpentry. Placing both hands upon the work table, he leaned forward and lowered his head.

"I have always been filled with the fires of the love of a God not old, and now to this has been joined the passion of the love of a young man. That love, dear earth, drives me to your salvation."

For a brief moment the carpenter closed his eyes; then, drawing into himself an unknown strength from some distant realm, he raised himself to his full stature and stepped out into the dusty street. With a gesture of finality he closed the door of his shop, turned, and spoke aloud.

"Well, brother John, it is time we met. I believe there is someone you wish to introduce to me."

CHAPTER 26

THE DESERT FLOOR WAS A FURNACE, the sun blinding in its brightness. Nonetheless, as far as the eye could see there were people. Some were standing, eyes closed. A few knelt. Many were weeping. Yet others, motionless, watched spellbound. All seemed oblivious to the scorching heat, their attention riveted on the fierce young prophet who stood upon a large rock in their midst. His voice rang like a silver trumpet, and as he spoke he turned, so that the fire of his gaze caught every eye.

For one brief moment his voice hesitated. It was something he thought he had seen at the edge of the crowd. Then, sure he had only imagined what he had so long hoped for, he continued. But there it was again—a light, too far back in the crowd for its source to be distinguished, but a light of unnatural origin. The desert prophet fell silent. He knew he was seeing what no other eye could see. He was seeing that for which he had been told to watch.

The light moved. It was coming toward the rocky mound.

Something–or someone–was out there, and upon that one the glory of God was resting.

The crowd grew uneasy and began turning in the direction of John's stare. For just an instant the man–whoever he was–broke into a small open space. Spontaneously John roared,

Behold!

Every eye now turned. Again the young man came into view, and shock swept across the face of the Baptizer.

What is this
that God has done!
My childhood friend,
my next of kin,
'tis Mary's son!

Now, eagerly and purposefully, John verily thundered.

Behold,
the Lamb of God!

The two men reached toward one another and embraced, but even as they did, the young carpenter kept them moving in the direction of the river.

"Come, brother John, today we have something here to fulfill."

"And what might that be?" asked John.

"All righteousness," replied the carpenter, stepping into the water's depths.

CHAPTER 27

"WHO WAS THAT MAN?" came a voice far out in the crowd.

"John, your words were strange. Are you not the Messiah?" came yet another inquiry.

Just in front of him stood two of his most zealous young disciples, their eyes still trying to keep in sight the young man who had so quickly disappeared beyond the crowd.

"John, please explain what just occurred," asked one of them, softly.

"No! I am *not* the Messiah!" rejoined the Baptizer. "Who, then, am I? I am the friend of the groom! I am come to introduce the groom–" He paused in mid-sentence, his right arm sweeping from one end of the throng to the other . . . "–to *his bride*!"

On hearing *this*, the two young men–who had thought they would be disciples of John until they drew their last breath–spontaneously turned and plunged into the crowd to follow the young Nazarene. They did not know this marked the first time since the Garden of Eden that man was seeking out God–to speak to him, unafraid, face to face.

CHAPTER 28

THE SPIRIT WITHIN HIM DROVE HIM OUT into the wasteland, past all villages, all nomads, all water, out to where blazing sun and burning sand drained away his strength.

"It is here she was tempted," he whispered as he cast his eyes across the endless dunes of sand.

"She lived with me, *here.* I provided her every need, yet she would have forsaken me for bread. She tried me . . . once and again she tempted me, even dared me. She preferred to worship a calf of gold than to deal with the greater task of worshiping a God she could not see."

He would have raised himself to a higher vantage point, but forty days without nourishment had taken a dreadful toll upon his body. The young carpenter collapsed and fell into the searing sand.

A few minutes later he woke with a start and struggled to his feet.

"There is someone here. Nearby! How could anyone find this forsaken place?"

In the distance he saw a beautiful, shimmering light–a light very definitely moving *toward* him, gliding smoothly over boulder and sand . . . as a serpent might glide across the earth.

"'Tis he!" cried the carpenter as he balanced himself and then ran, unhesitatingly, toward the glowing figure. The distance separating them diminished quickly as they approached one another. Suddenly, both paused. Like two gladiators they circled, each eyeing the other in wonder.

So this is the one who came to my ancestor, Adam! thought the carpenter as he searched out every feature of the beautiful creature before him.

So this is God . . . in human form! cried the other to himself, hardly able to hide his bitter joy! *God, visible! God, locatable! God, here, in dimension, space, and time! God, on* my *planet! God, incarnate inside the flimsy protection of blood, bone, and skin! God,* vulnerable*!*

God–killable*!* he almost cried aloud.

Never had the adversary dared dream of such a dark and wondrous opportunity!

The fallen archangel at last broke the silence. His voice was enchanting, containing all the loveliness of the spheres.

"Sooo," he sang. "So, the one claiming to be the Son of God."

"I am Jesus of Nazareth. A carpenter by trade. Born of woman."

"Are you not the Son of God?" demanded the shimmering creature. With those words–and that challenge–the angel of light reached down and cradled a large, smooth stone in his hand.

"You are hungry! Weak unto *death*," he continued, biting out the last word. "If you are the Son of God, here! Turn this stone to bread and *eat*!"

The young carpenter stared long at the stone.

So this is how it feels to be a man tempted–face to face–by the tempter. So this is how my creation, Adam, felt that day in the garden. Ah, and here I am now, receiving the same temptation Israel did when she was in the selfsame desert . . . lo, even in this very place!

As the young man stared at the stone, he felt the ache in his belly, the renewed spasms in his legs. Then, lifting his head and looking full face into the eyes of the waiting angel, he wavered. He was *feeling* temptation now, and he knew it. From deep within his bosom he began to recall the ancient times. Heard *his* own words! Strength surged out of his Spirit into his body!

"Lucifer! Have you forgotten? It is I who recorded it! '*Man* shall not live by bread alone.'

"*Man* shall *live*! He shall live. . . ." The carpenter moved his hand toward his own bosom. "Man shall live by *every* word that is spoken from the mouth of God!"

A moment of rage flickered across the face of the angel. Then, smiling gently, he raised his hand. Instantly the scene changed, and the two were standing atop the highest pinnacle of the Temple. The carpenter was poised precariously at its edge.

"If you are the Son of *God*, jump . . . from *here*! You know full well it is written that God will command *his* angels to guard you. *They* will not allow you to strike the stone below," he continued sweetly. "The angels will bear you up."

The carpenter eyed the dazzling heights. His weakened frame began to collapse under him. But in the same instant the unseen realm opened before him. It was true–he could see them–a legion of angels were poised to lunge forth at his slightest word.

Again his mind raced back to Israel. So often she had dared question his care for her. Again, his own words welled up from within his inmost being. His knees braced. Boldly, even serenely, he turned.

"Lucifer, have you forgotten? I have recorded it: 'You shall not tempt the Lord, *your* God.'"

The archangel, caught off guard by so sure a response, was dazed by the carpenter's words. For an instant his own knees, which in a bygone age had so often bent to his God, momentarily buckled. Quickly he jerked himself free of this brief sanity and raised his hand again.

Once more the scene changed.

They were now on some high mountain overlooking the whole world. Below them, glistening in garland beauty, were all the great kingdoms of the past; beside them the kingdoms of the present. Beyond them, plainly visible out there in the future, were kingdoms yet unknown. Some were glorious, some powerful, others sparkling in splendor.

"You have come, *I* know why," hissed the angel. "You have come to rule the land! To rule earth. Then let us make short work of your task. You know that all kingdoms upon earth–past, present, and future–are mine and mine alone. All governments are *mine*!" The angel paused, giving full opportunity for a rejoinder.

The carpenter chose not to challenge a statement both knew to be true. The angel moved very close, his words sounding like the chimes of heaven.

"I will give to you these kingdoms, *all* of them! You may rule them all–and this whole planet with them! They are not only mine, but I may *give* them . . . to whomever I please."

Again the carpenter disputed not the angel's words.

"I will give them all . . . to you. You need do but one thing, and one thing only: Fall down here . . . now . . . and worship *me*!"

The young man looked again at the kingdoms. Every fiber in his being ached. He was weary beyond words. Tired, terribly tired. The task before him seemed so wearisome, so unutterably difficult, with a price to be paid that seemed, for a moment, far too great.

But once more the young man bolted upright. Something he had said to Israel long ago began singing within his depths.

Be gone, Satan!
It has been recorded,
"You shall worship the Lord,
your God!
You will serve him . . . him,
alone!"

The angel quaked in astonishment at so strong a rejoinder. For an instant his body spasmed, his face contracted, the light of his being dimmed. Slowly he willed back his strength, the glow of his light brightening once more.

"I shall leave you . . . for the moment."

At the very instant the fallen archangel vanished, a company of elect angels appeared, even as their Lord crumpled upon the rocks.

After a few moments of angelic care, the perilously weak man opened his eyes. A smile broke across his blistered face; words formed upon his cracked lips.

Did you see?
I ask,
Did you see!

The angels nodded an embarrassed assent.

"Did you see!" he cried again, struggling to his feet. "I beat him! Neither was the garden scene nor Israel's fate repeated here, this day. It was a *man* who lost to Satan in the Garden that day. This time Satan lost. And he lost to a *man*! He lost to me, not as God. He lost to me . . . as man! As surely as he once beguiled man, today he lost . . . to . . . a . . . *man*!"

The carpenter staggered toward a rock, while angels, quite unaccustomed to such unprecedented behavior, stepped back. The man from Nazareth braced himself against a boulder, raised his head toward a starry, moonlit sky, and cried aloud,

"I beat him. I, Jesus of Nazareth, beat him."

Now standing erect, he threw his head heavenward and cried again.

Soon–
Yes, soon now–
Very, very soon!

CHAPTER 29

"TO A WEDDING?"

"Yes, I am going to a wedding in Cana," replied his mother. "They are friends of mine. They have asked that I also invite you."

"To a wedding . . ." He repeated the words, slowly. "Yes, it is a matter to consider; after all, I came to earth for a . . ." His words ended there, but his mother understood.

That evening at the appointed time, Mary departed for the wedding without her son, as he was deep in consultation with that small band of men who followed him.

Later that evening he made his way to the little village where his mother had earlier gone, pensively wandering its narrow streets, watching the people making their way home from a day's work, listening to the conversations coming from within the houses, observing the creaking carts coming back from the marketplace. Everyone, it seemed to him, appeared so tired, their countenances so very empty. Joy seemed to have departed this place. Everything, in *his* eyes, appeared so *old.*

His ears caught the sound of festivity. *The wedding. There will be joy enough there.* His pace quickened.

It was through a small entrance in the rear that the young carpenter entered the wedding hall, very late and quite unnoticed. He made his way to an obscure place far to the back of the crowded room and began observing the proceedings of the evening with unusual interest.

At the center of the festivities was a huge banquet table, laden with all manner of delightful foods. There was the groom, so young, and his bride, so beautiful. Both were obviously very much in love. And, truly, the room was filled with an atmosphere of joy.

Mary was speaking with the young couple. Just as she was about to turn away, he noticed that the groom was called aside by two very worried looking servants.

So this is how it is. Multitudes here. The beautiful bride, the bridegroom. The wine. Yes, so it will be when I . . .

His thoughts were intruded upon by some deeper scene *within* him. He looked again at the hall and the wedding guests. The divine eyes within him began looking past the crowded room, to some larger scene. There was a crowd, yes, but it was the whole host of fallen mankind. Faces were sad, voices tired, witnessing to what was in the heart. Oldness hung in the air. The young carpenter sighed deeply, growing sad at the melancholy sight his inner eye beheld.

A gentle and familiar voice seemed to be calling him back to his earthly surroundings. For an instant he found himself watching both scenes at once–one, a whole world, the other, a local wedding. So different, yet so alike.

"They are out of wine!" came a voice.

It was his mother.

"Yes, I know," he said, increased in sadness by the view of his double scene and her pronouncement, so correct in its assessment.

Mary was accustomed to these interludes when his spirit and

mind met between two realms. She paused a moment and repeated softly, "They are out of wine."

He turned and looked at her, the vision of a sad world still lingering in his sight . . . a world so desperately in need of redemptive joy.

"Woman, do you know what you are asking of me? My time has not yet come!"

"I know," she whispered again, reassuringly. "Still, right now, *this* wedding is out of wine!" And with that she turned away, missing the soft smile that broke upon his face. Mary crossed the room to the groom and his two distraught servants. "I believe you are out of wine, are you not?"

"Yes, we are. And there is none to be found in all the village. We have searched everywhere. It seems the whole world is out of wine."

"I offer this suggestion, then," she replied. "Do you see the young man over there, the one sitting in the farthest corner?"

The face of one of the servants grew ashen. "Oh, my . . . I did not know *he* was here. It is the carpenter turned prophet. Oh, my!"

"Go to him. Whatever he tells you to do, do it!"

The two servants exchanged puzzled glances. One shrugged his shoulders, and with that the two men began moving cautiously across the hall.

"Uh, sir. We . . . we are out of wine."

"Yes, I know. You have been out of wine for a long, long time."

Once more the two men exchanged looks of consternation.

"Sir, what shall we do? There must be wine at the close; it is a custom."

"A good custom indeed," said the carpenter. "What you need is a new wine. The *best* wine, saved for the very *last*! Do you see those six large pots over there?"

"Yes, but sir, we cannot use those pots. They are for the rite of purification; they are for the dead."

"Go. Fill those pots with water. After that, take what comes from them to the director of the wedding. He will tell you what to do."

The servants stared. "Sir . . . ?"

"Go."

"Yes, sir."

As the servants turned, one murmured aloud, "Pots of death. What does he expect to come out of the likes of them?"

For a long time the young carpenter continued to watch. His mind and heart were fertile with thoughts–thoughts similar, perhaps, to those of any young man on such an occasion, contemplating his own future wedding plans.

The festivities had obviously been drawing to a close, but now a new energy, a new delight, was making its way across the room. Something had sparked the revelry in everyone. And why not? After all, they now had 150 gallons of *delicious* new wine!

The Nazarene carpenter slipped from the crowded room, unnoticed, and once more stepped out into Cana's night. He paused for a moment, his attention drawn to a conversation taking place at the door of the banquet hall. It was the wedding director bidding good night to some of the guests.

"Never, in all my years," said he. "Never! Always before, the groom waits until the end and brings out the worst wine! In many a case, I tell you, no wine at all would have been better. But tonight–ah, tonight! At the very end–at the *end*, mind you–the groom brought out the best wine I have ever tasted here or anywhere. Wine," he laughed, "the likes of which has not been served since the dawn of creation.

"What an idea! The best wine, at the very end. What a *glorious* idea!"

CHAPTER 30

"WHAT DID HE SAY TO ME WHEN FIRST I MET HIM?" responded the Levite to his friend Jude, as the two men moved slowly along with the throng.

"I was sitting at a table collecting taxes. No, that is not exactly accurate. Actually, business was slow, as it often is with tax collectors, so I was using my time to memorize a list!"

"A list?" rejoined Jude.

"Yes. I have memorized dozens of them. Mostly laws. You know, do this, do not do this; this is a sin, this is not. This is right, that is wrong! You see, I had an ambition. Oh, what an ambition! To know every law of our religion. To know every rule there was to know and to keep them *all*!"

Matthew ended his words with a hearty laugh.

"Anyway, I was sitting there when along came a crowd of people . . . one very much like this one. Such a commotion, and I wondered for what. Then I saw. Ah, it was *he*! He walked over to where I sat, stared at me, or right through me, and then said:

Matthew, I will fulfill
your laws. I will destroy the rules.
Now come, follow me.

Matthew laughed again. "Now I keep a new list."

"You do?" said his surprised friend. "Of what?"

"I keep a list of all the things he has said he would fulfill, do away with, abolish, void, bring down, conclude, destroy, or annihilate! It grows, I might add, almost daily."

Jude smiled. "May I impose on you and ask to hear the contents of *this* list? Dare I call such a thing a list? It sounds more like the roll call of Judgment Day."

"Let us see," responded Matthew enthusiastically. "So far, of things marked for obliteration, I have the law, rules, Satan (if you please) and his angelic host, demons, governments, the world's system. Mind you this one: all realms seen and unseen. In fact, as best I can understand him, the . . . well, the entire cosmos. And then there are the Sabbath, holy days, rituals, the Temple, observances, sin, creation, and . . ."

The two men stopped, as had the crowd around them. Something up ahead was now obstructing their path. Whatever it was, the young carpenter was taking an exceptional interest in it.

"See that look on his face, Matthew? Well, I have seen it before, on rare occasions. All memorable, I might add. And unless I miss a fair guess, you are going to be adding to that list of yours quite soon."

CHAPTER 31

OUT OF THE CITY OF NAIN, moving toward a burial ground, came a moaning, wailing procession. At the first sight of it, the carpenter had come to a sudden stop. The beating drums, the cadence of the clattering sticks, and the cry of the professional wailer held him almost spellbound. Or perhaps it was not these at all that so firmly held his attention. Was it, rather, something he was viewing that no mortal eye could see?

There was a woman in the procession, a widow. Following behind her were four men. Upon their shoulders rested a bier, cradling the lifeless form of a young boy. But was there more?

Yes, there was something else, but only those who see the unseen could know of its presence. *He* could see, and what he saw provoked first his interest, then his highest rage.

Upon the bier, dark and dreadful, stood the angel of death, holding the little boy fast within his cold domain.

The carpenter raised his hand. Time stood still. The two–the carpenter and the death angel–now stood alone, in realms spiritual. Thc young Nazarene, almost mad with rage, moved quickly toward the dark angel.

"You!" cried Death, in stunned amazement.

The carpenter shook his head slowly, for it was a grotesque and hideous thing that was standing before him. He sighed, and thought within,

Can it be
that I
who made the lamb
made thee?

"We have met before," spoke the carpenter aloud, a hint of challenge in his voice.

"Yes," came the gurgling voice of Death. "You prevented me from my appointed task, and held from me my rightful prey that night. Ah, but here, today, you are too late, Son of God! See! This one is *already* mine. Even now my domain is his abode . . . and *none* can tread there. Nothing," roared the dark angel, "no power, no hope, no dream, no prayer can reach him now! This is not as it was when last we met in Egypt on the first night of Passover. . . . *This* time you have come too late!"

Death's cold glare was returned by eyes blazing with unmitigated rage. Rage so great that even Death shuddered at the sight of such unbridled fury.

"You know not all things, immortal Death," replied the young carpenter, as he spoke through clenched teeth.

The young man raised his hand again. Time's scene reappeared. Quickly the carpenter walked to the middle of the road; the funeral processional came to an abrupt halt. The four men, a little uncertain of what was happening, lowered the bier to the ground. A crowd of people, and all their thoughts, stood still at the sight of a man so utterly consumed with livid rage.

The carpenter knelt beside the child, reaching out his hand to touch him. A cry went up from the child's mother. "Lord, touch him not, for it is written we are not to touch the uncleanness of death."

The young man raised his head, narrowed his eyes upon the dark angel, and replied, "Death? What death?"

The death angel sneered, bent low, and tightened his grip upon the child.

Ever so gently the kneeling carpenter continued moving his hand toward the boy. As the carpenter's hand reached, not the child, but the hand of Death, the dark angel screamed in astonishment, tearing his hand away in frothing agony. The crowd broke out in wild cries of fear and joy. The young boy opened his eyes and sat up.

While chaotic ecstasy reigned over the crowd, the young carpenter moved swiftly down the road to intercept again that black and terrible creature who bore the name Azell.

"Halt!" thundered the Lord as he stepped past time and entered again the unseen realms.

For the first time since he had been loosed upon creation that awful day in the garden, the angel of death obeyed the command of another.

"Death! Damned Death," cried the Lord, now at the very edge of self-control. "Hear me, Death! Damned . . . doomed . . . Death! Ere my bride appears upon the scene . . . you, Azell . . . you, Death . . . *you* shall die!"

The young carpenter turned away. Upon his face, where rage had burned in full fury but a moment before, there was now the serene glow of triumph.

"Matthew."

"Yes, I know, Jude," replied the Levite, fumbling through the pockets of his cloak. "Now where *did* I put that list?"

CHAPTER 32

THE CARPENTER WAS VERY TIRED; the day had been long and trouble filled. If he did not hurry, he would be late for a banquet being given in his honor, but the crowd pressed in against him from all sides. Movement in this melee was difficult at best.

Above the din that rose around him came another sound–one not natural to this realm.

It came again–a long, mournful wail. All other voices fell silent, all eyes searched for the source of this eerie chant. A song out of hell it was, piercing the bravest soul with icy fear. Children ran away, some people covered their ears, while others drew their garments tightly about them.

The young carpenter responded instantly, forcing his way through a human sea toward the ghastly cry. His very demeanor caused a path in the crowd to open before him, revealing at its edge a strange creature from whom rose the fiendish music.

Suddenly her wailing stopped. In its place came hard, labored breathing interspersed with snarls and whines. Her long hair hung so tangled about her head and shoulders it was not clear which direction she faced.

Then, from beneath that matted mess, she thrust forth two defiant hands, clawlike, with which she jerked back her hair, revealing a blurred and twisted face. A sick groan went up from the crowd. Her face was filthy, her eyes glazed. She turned toward the sun, searching its fire as one attempting to find a way back to reality.

The carpenter stepped in her path, his shadow falling upon her face. She whimpered, then struggled, obviously trying again–vainly–to pull herself free of something . . . to understand . . . anything.

Her glazed eyes met his. She twisted for a brief instant, then a hideous, wicked smile grew upon her face. The wail began again–this time higher, more obscene than before. Her dark music would drop, then rise again, a demonic psalm celebrating some perverse triumph. Its wretched cadence was somehow flaunting that triumph at the young Nazarene.

The carpenter knew the meaning of the wail. He knew its source, and he knew it was the bondage which held this girl that was being so gleefully trumpeted.

Who was this girl?

The very daughter of Israel–the offspring of a whore.

As her mother had been, so was she. Her mother had gone into sin with Egypt and Babylon; so also had the daughter followed willingly in her mother's steps.

While only a child, this one had been willful, headstrong, and rebellious. When she discovered that men lusted after her body, she was both intoxicated with a sense of power and filled with bitter contempt toward her suitors. She gave her body at first, but as she grew older and wiser, she placed a price upon it. Contempt grew deeper, rebellion more violent, yet she gloried in her sin and wore with pride the title of harlot. Little by little the dark forces of the netherworld made home in her fleshly being.

"Truly, the daughter of Jeru," sighed the Galilean.

The wail subsided; again the girl struggled against some unseen force. Then came a sneer, followed by a laugh–a defiant, derisive laugh, aimed straight at the prophet from Galilee.

Every eye that watched seemed to understand that something–or someone–within her was making sport of the young prophet, though the point of the taunt was unclear.

Pity, anger, and understanding welled up from within the Nazarene. But more. Springing first from his heart, then surging across his face, was the unmistakable look of love!

What was it about this prostitute that so captured the Lord's attention?

A high moment in divine history was about to unfold.

The carpenter searched the young girl's face. He looked past the wild, hollow eyes. He saw the loneliness, the pain, the scars, the aged look upon one so young. He saw the hurt, the sense of betrayal; he saw the frantic terror that even now gripped her heart, and heard again the muted cry for help.

He looked past the outward horror, the cynicism, the cuts, the snarls and growls, the heinous laughter. He saw the demon in her–no, seven demons. He saw the soul, dark, in need of redemption. But deeper still penetrated his divine gaze! He saw the human spirit–a lifeless, gray thing. The human spirit–an element found in the bosom of every human being, yet belonging to the heavenly realm–lying there, cold and dead since the days of fallen Adam.

Looking yet deeper, he saw something else. A beautiful, beautiful young girl. But was this possible?

He raised his hand.

The young carpenter no longer saw the girl or the crowd around them. He was looking back into eternity, even to the age before the eternals, to a moment known to no other–that moment when he had marked off portions of his own divine nature . . . had marked them off that they might one day be portions of . . .

He saw it! A portion of his being that had been the very *first* to be marked off.

He dropped his hand. He looked again at that dead spirit within the girl.

Her spirit is ***destined***
*to be made alive–**again!***
Marked off ***in*** *me,*
before the foundation of the age.
Determined, even then,
that ***this one*** *would become . . .*

Something in the young girl sensed the intensity of his searching gaze. Falling back, the girl began to howl and snap. Her rage and cursing spiraled into madness.

The carpenter responded instantly. Thrusting out his hand, he pointed directly at the girl. In an earthshaking voice that reverberated like a thunderclap, he cried,

She is not yours!
Leave her.
Come out!
Now and forever.

The young girl's body contorted, her eyes filled with terror. She clutched her head as in some indescribable pain. The obscene wail lifted from her. The girl let out a soul-freezing scream and crumpled to the ground. There was no doubt in anyone's mind. The girl was dead.

Instinctively, several women rushed to where the young girl's lifeless body had fallen. They pulled back her hair and stared in dumbfounded amazement.

The girl was asleep, a faint hint of tranquil peace upon her face.

And while no one was noticing, the young carpenter stole away, almost tardy now for a dinner engagement.

And the girl, left lying there on the ground . . . who is she?

Who, *really*, is this girl?

CHAPTER 33

THE WEALTHIEST MAN IN THE CITY, and a Pharisee–rich and religious. Such would be the carpenter's host this evening.

He was greeted at the door of the luxurious mansion by a well-dressed servant who quickly ushered him through the home and out into a large, open garden. Not far away, on the city wall, the outline of the watchman's turret could be seen under a moonlit sky.

Spread out on the ground at the center of the garden was a vast tapestry covered with an endless array of exotic foods. Everywhere, it seemed, servants were scurrying about, some leading guests to their appointed place, others bringing more huge trays of delicacies into the garden.

Among the guests present were the leading citizens of the city.

Simon, standing at the rear of the garden, motioned for the young prophet to come and take the *second*-highest place of honor in the banquet room. The host then rang a small bell. Following their host's example, everyone knelt and then reclined and started eating.

There was music, wine, laughter, and an atmosphere of relaxed revelry. All evidence pointed to a delightful evening with a wealthy host and a famous young prophet. Perhaps there might even be a time for addressing questions to the honored guest. But such would not be the turn of things.

Only a few minutes into the meal there was a commotion at the door, enough to catch the attention of a few eyes, which in turn provoked a flurry of whispers. In a moment the garden was dead silent. Standing in the doorway was a woman of the street. The loudest sound now was the strained breathing of a hundred souls. From somewhere came the words,

It is a whore!

Simon was mortified. Such an intrusion, by a woman of the street, here . . . in *his* home. With *this* guest present. Unbelievable.

For a long moment, the young girl stood motionless in the doorway. All knew her, and some marveled that she was neither afraid nor ashamed. She seemed, rather, almost serene.

They wondered when that shrill, unearthly wail would commence, but some observed that she seemed changed in every way.

The Galilean guest, in the meantime, continued eating, not even bothering to look up.

The young girl began moving. The electric tension in the room soared, for there was no doubt as to her destination. Every eye watched, transfixed, as the young girl moved across the garden and took her place just behind the young prophet, even at his feet.

Turning to look over his shoulder, the young man acknowledged the girl's presence for the first time. For an incredibly long moment nothing in the room moved.

Then the girl pulled from her cloak a beautiful vase, obviously filled with some exotic and terribly expensive oil, its contents undoubtedly representing her whole life's possessions. With uncommon grace and a dignity bordering on regality, she broke open one end of the vase and slipped to her knees. The garden was immediately filled with a rich, intoxicating scent of exotic perfume.

Simon stared, horrified, trying not to believe that an unclean woman was such a short distance from him *and* at the very feet of the young prophet. He turned to one of the dignitaries and said in a whisper that was meant to be heard, "Surely, if this man is a prophet, he knows she is a street woman, defiled! Surely he will not allow her to touch him."

Yet others whispered loudly, "Surely she will not touch *him.* He is a man of God!" The young girl began to pour the precious oil upon the feet of the carpenter. As she did, she lifted first her face, and then a hand, heavenward, while hot tears poured softly down her face. Soon the tears were falling upon his feet, mingling with the oil.

The carpenter made no protest, nor did he stir.

A murmur of shocked disbelief filled the room as the woman of sin began to bathe his feet with oil and tears. Reaching down, she lovingly–even passionately–began kissing his feet.

And from the city walls the watchman of the night called out the evening psalm:

Thou shalt
love the Lord
thy God
with all thy soul,
and all thy heart,
and all thy might.

But *no one* seemed to have heard. And those who heard did not understand.

Now, taking the tresses of her long and beautiful hair, the young girl wrapped them tightly together, forming them into a towel, and began to wipe his feet. She wiped them dry–except for her newest tears.

Who, pray tell, is this incredible young girl?

CHAPTER 34

"SIMON."

The young prophet broke his silence in a quiet, disconcertingly calm voice.

"Simon, you are a man who cares for the things of God. You have given this banquet in my honor, have you not?"

"Yes, that is true."

"When I came into your home, Simon, there was no kiss of greeting upon my cheek; no servant washed from my feet the dirt of this day. But this woman whom you have called a woman of sin has come and washed my feet, not with water, but with the costliest of oils . . . and with her tears. Further, she has kissed them dry with her lips.

"Now, Simon, I have a question for you. Two men owed great debts to a king, but one owed a greater sum. The king forgave them both their debts. Which one, Simon, do you suppose loved the king the more?"

Simon had turned a bright crimson in anger and embarrassment. He bit off every word of his reply.

"Well, Lord, the one who owed the greater debt, I suppose."

"You have spoken the truth, Simon."

The young prophet stood, and as he did, he faced the girl. He reached out his hand and lifted her to her feet.

"Truly, the one forgiven little, loves little. The one forgiven much, loves much." He stared straight at the young girl . . . whose face had become a river of sparkling tears.

"You are forgiven and cleansed. All is past, as though it never had been."

The young girl looked at him as though she understood the furthest depths of his every word.

"Now, child, go . . . and sin no more."

The young girl did not move. Rather, she dropped, once more, to her knees.

"My Lord, and my God. I am cleansed . . . and I shall sin no more. But I shall never . . . never . . . go away."

CHAPTER 35

ABOUT TWENTY MEN AND FOUR WOMEN accompanied him wherever he traveled. From the day of her deliverance, she did not ask; she simply *became* part of that little band of followers. Wherever he went, she went, and poured out her whole love and her whole life on him.

In the earliest hours of the morning she could be found preparing his breakfast. When he sat down to teach, *she* was there, at his feet. When he departed, she departed with him. When those twenty men asked too much of him, she quietly, firmly, protested. She washed his feet, served his meals, cared for his clothes, placed fruit beside his bed in the evenings. He who said of himself, "I am the living water," always had cool water to drink–brought by *her* hands. When nights were cold, she made sure the house where he was guested would be warm. In the hot, blistering sun of summer, she walked with the little band of followers, village to village, city to city–always following *him*.

Why such devotion?

Because she adored him. Fervently, single-mindedly, she loved him. She was totally enamored, completely enraptured, and utterly in love with her Lord and Master. She did not care who knew it. She was embarrassingly unembarrassed about the matter.

The others eventually grew used to the sight of her single-minded adoration and her uninhibited outpouring of affection, which continued unceasingly from earliest dawn to the last light of night.

They even learned from her. Oh, they *all* professed a love for him that was equal to hers. But they *spoke* of overthrowing Rome, of abolishing the present Hebrew state, of setting up a spectacular throne, of avenging the vicious rumors that seemed always to be spread about concerning their Lord. They dreamed of wielding both political and spiritual power, of casting out demons, of throwing Caesar into a dungeon and Satan into a burning pit.

They professed love, but talked power and fame. Little by little they changed. As months turned to years, they spoke less of conquest and got down to the business of loving their God.

The most amazing thing of all was this: He responded. He poured out love in return. It seemed a little odd, the Son of God, caring, affectionate, loving, and returning love . . . so profoundly, so totally. That God might love, with such ardor, was simply something that had never occurred to them. Nor could they quite understand why they found it so difficult to express love toward him.

Her mother before her had failed at this same simple matter for centuries, but now, before all eyes, this simple girl was unfolding the highest order of the universe. To *love* her God.

Watching her, they learned. For though she expressed her love in service and care, she expressed her love yet more in eyes, in heart, in soul, and in the fervor and passion of her whole being. No abstraction, this love. An unnerving thing this. Unwavering, day after day, with total abandon–loving him. You saw it in her eyes, in her kneeling, in moments of praise and rejoicing, and when she looked into his face–which was almost always.

Who is this girl . . . this *incredible* girl?

CHAPTER 36

THAT ANCIENT SENSE OF ALONENESS had gripped him once more. Slipping away from everyone, he left the city and slowly made his way up the slopes of the Mount of Olives. At a good vantage point he stopped, knelt, and leaned back on one of the trees, there to view the city across the valley before him.

He had watched this city for over two thousand years; and for as many years she had broken his heart. He sighed, pressed his chin into his hands, and began to weep.

His gaze intensified, and the sight of the city below gave way to a divine sight. Slowly the city of people, houses, and Temple drew together as one. Out from this swirling mosaic began to emerge a single form. In the place of the city there appeared, standing in the valley across from him, a young and very beautiful woman. She was robed all in white.

He uttered but one word,

Jeru.

She was very young, and utterly beautiful. As he looked at her, he recalled how she had come into this, the land of promise, and how she had made her home in the heartland of Judea. In those days her beauty and her innocence were breathtaking. Nonetheless, from the outset, she seemed to show an inordinate curiosity toward the strange ways of the people and gods of the surrounding lands. In the days of Solomon, at the zenith of her beauty, she broke her vows of betrothal with him and flung herself into *their* world.

For a long time he gazed at the girl, and as the minutes passed, the young girl seemed to grow older. Her features hardened, as did her heart.

He knew. Soon she would join with others in killing the very One to whom she had been betrothed. But more. He knew very soon that Jeru would also *die*! Die, never to rise again.

Not only she, but all those who had enticed her from him.

My rivals, my enemies—all will soon come to an end. In her place will arise a spiritual being of whom you, Jeru, have been but a picture. Another will come, far more beautiful than you. A new—

But his thoughts were abruptly interrupted.

"My Lord, I would not have disturbed you, but it is important—very important."

"Yes?"

"We have wind of a plot. Of the details we are uncertain, but it appears someone . . ."

"Yes, I know. I have known for a long, long time. Do not concern yourself. It is a matter being carefully watched by my Father. Now, may I ask a favor? Would you wait for me at the base of the mount? I would be alone for a moment longer."

"Yes, Lord," responded the disciple, turning to make a hasty retreat from the hill's summit.

Again he turned his eye back to the city below. The awful realization of what this ancient city really was engulfed him again. Through gushing tears and sobs of sorrow, he cried out.

"O Jerusalem, Jerusalem. You have so often stoned the very ones who came to save you. How often have they called you . . . have I called you . . . to return. But you would not. How oft would I have taken you in my arms as a hen does her brood, but you would not."

O, Jeru,
Jeru, Jerusalem,
Tonight, seal your fate . . . forever.

CHAPTER 37

LATER THAT NIGHT A LONELY FIGURE WAS led from his place of prayer in an olive grove to the hall of judgment, there to be tried for blasphemy against God. A few had loved him, but many more had hated him.

The midnight trial made that fact evident. His words were twisted; false witnesses reported to the city fathers the words that had to be said. The point in it all was obvious. They did not want this troublesome Galilean to exist any longer.

"This one is not worthy of life." That was the final verdict. He was led from the hall to his appointment with death.

Strange, is it not, what sometimes crosses the mind of a man facing death. He was recalling a moment in the distant past. A conversation.

"Adam, do you see this seed? Within me, and within this seed, is a principle that cannot be rescinded. If the seed lives . . . it abides *alone.* But if the seed falls into the ground and dies . . .

"Sleep here, Adam. Or abide alone forever! *Live*, in aloneness. *Die*, and become many."

His thoughts were interrupted. It seems there had been a slight oversight. He would have to be tried again.

CHAPTER 38

ENEMY OCCUPATION OF THE LAND NECESSITATED a trial by the foreign government. The government of the Hebrews *and* the heathen government would have to be in agreement to end this man. Jew and Gentile must be one in this matter. And so they led him to Pilate's palace.

The carpenter observed carefully the face of the man who would try to rescue from execution an innocent victim who did not choose to be rescued.

The conversation between them touched on many things, including government.

"Before this day ends," the carpenter told him matter-of-factly, "*both* your governments, and *both* your races, will be executed with me. Hebrews and heathen will cease to exist."

With that comment, Pilate ordered the young prophet returned to his enemies.

Earthly governments had now agreed: He must die. But one

more vote was needed for total unanimity. And so the citizens of the city were brought together to express their verdict.

The Galilean was led onto a balcony overlooking a vast courtyard. The citizens of Jerusalem were there, as far as the eye could see, shouting and screaming. His eyes blurred; the crowd before him began to spin in his vision. Slowly the scene re-formed.

Before him stood his betrothed, Jeru. She raised her fist and shook it at him. Contempt and rage glowering in her face, she cried out her sentiments. "Away with him! Crucify him. Crucify him!" she demanded.

He turned his head and shut his eyes, trying to blot out the sight of hate so absolute. But she would make her choice clear. She cried again, "Crucify him! Crucify him!"

From deep within his being he groaned,

O, Jeru, Jeru–Jerusalem!

The verdict complete, the soldiers of heathendom now led their victim out of the court, into the street, and to an awaiting prison. Through dark chambers they led him, stripped him, and beat him . . . mercilessly.

For a moment he lost consciousness. When he awoke, he–as earth's first man once had done–instinctively reached for his side.

"No. Not yet. I am still whole."

He rolled over on the cold stone floor, tried to rise, but collapsed from pain. Between swollen lips he whispered,

Not yet, Adam. Not yet. But soon.

CHAPTER 39

HALF BLIND, NEAR DEATH, he dragged the wooden beam up the loathsome hill. When he stumbled, a passerby was conscripted to complete the task.

Through blood-filled eyes he caught his first glimpse of Golgotha and heard the sound of hammers finishing their instrument of execution.

The soldiers turned the carpenter around so he might see what lay upon the ground before him.

The cross!

He had not seen it since *that* day . . . the day before the birth of eternity.

"The greatest instrument of destruction in the universe!" he whispered. He raised his bruised head and groped–with eyes nearly blind–to see if all else was in place. Yes, there the nails, the mallet, the derisive sign, the gall. All were present, having been inseparably linked to him for unnumbered ages.

Again he cast his eyes down at the cross lying before him. None on earth nor in the skies could e'er have guessed that beam of wood constituted the force that would annihilate the whole of creation.

But something was missing!

Slowly he looked about, surveying the whole macabre panorama. There it was! In the hands of a Roman soldier. The spear that would open his side.

Something within him, a sense of completion, filled his being. A soft smile struggled to the surface of his swollen face.

"On with it. Crucify him!" someone in the crowd screamed.

"Oh, you have no idea what shall be crucified this day," he murmured. Then, turning his eyes heavenward, he whispered again, addressing universes unseen, "All things are ready."

With that simple word the whole habitation of heavenly places emptied, as the angelic host hurled itself into time, there to fill every roof, hill, and mountain in and around Jerusalem. Ten thousand times ten thousand swords were drawn by outraged and weeping angels. Every sinew in them strained, waiting for a command–any command–that would allow them to unleash vengeance upon that hill.

Pitilessly the soldiers began to shove him down upon the beam of wood, only to discover his utter willingness to lie down upon this cross and stretch out his hands and feet. Nor did it escape their eyes that their captive opened his palms to the waiting nails.

One of the soldiers, hesitating for only a moment as he contemplated this strange man before him, reached for one of the long, cold spikes and the heavy iron mallet. He pressed the nail hard against the wrist and raised his hammer high into the air.

The carpenter raised his other hand slightly, and *space and time stood still*!

Within the very core of the spirits of every angel, bursting like fire, came the unspoken, and quite unbelievable, command of their Lord. For a single instant they hesitated.

"Now!" commanded the carpenter. "*All* things to the cross!"

CHAPTER 40

THE YOUNG CARPENTER HAD GIVEN the angels not only a command but an ability. They could do something that, until now, only *he* had ever done. To accomplish his will he had now allowed his angels to become masters of space and time. They would know what only *I AM* had ever known before: For the next few moments they would be able to move to any point in time, space . . . or eternity. They could roam the corridors of universal time, breaking into any place in history. They could travel across all points of time–and to *many* places in eternity–moving, if necessary, in *both* directions of eternity, even to the age before the ages and, if need be, to the final end of all ages.

Hurtling faster than even they could conceive, each went to his appointed place to perform his Master's will.

CHAPTER 41

IT WAS THE ANGEL WHO BORE the simple name Messenger who plunged backward through all time, then back through all eternity past–even to that age before *all* things, *save God*! There, in eternity past, he found a lamb–slain–upon a wooden cross. Lifting high this trophy of endless love–a trophy, a death, a crucifixion unknown until now–he bore the slain lamb forward through eternity into time, and finally to Golgotha, there to make that cross–and lamb–one with the cursed tree and the carpenter who lay outstretched upon it. All points of time past and time future, all points of eternity past and eternity future, converged on that cross. A cross, and its crucified victim, slain before creation, had finally found its place in the continuum of time. And all things that had been crucified before the foundation of the world journeyed to Golgotha–from out of the past and from out of the future–to be crucified in *time*!

Yet another angel went to that long-forgotten place where Eve and Seth had once laid the body of an ancient Adam. The angel clutched into his arms the firstborn of our race, and bore him forward through time, coming at last to Calvary.

Within the very bosom of Adam lay all the descendants of the human race, for they were–after all–*in* him. Further, in the bosom of that first man lay not only all mankind but also the Adamic fall, the curse, and the self-nature that had invaded, plundered, and twisted man's soul.

Adam, and all mankind *in* him, was carried in angelic hands to the place of the carpenter's execution, and there became one with the cross. Adam's race was crucified!

One of the archangels rose from earth's plane, stood above this planet, and called to time past and time future, commanding all governments, rules, dominions, and principalities from all earth's ages to come forth. Capturing them all in his mighty arms, he swept back into time's sphere and made flight toward Jerusalem. Standing before the cross, he waited . . . waited to see princes and principalities crucified upon the cross of our Lord!

But one of the angels did not stir from his place. Golgotha itself was his appointment. On one side of the cross stood a crowd of Hebrews. On the other side, a garrison of Gentile soldiers. Between them, seen only by eyes that belonged to the unseen, was a wall. An insurmountable wall dividing Jew and Gentile, having kept them separated since the days of Abraham. Wrestling the wall into his powerful arms, the angel lifted that barrier up, paused before the cross, and waited . . . waited to see crucified upon the cross the dividing wall between the circumcised and the uncircumcised.

He waited, as did the others, for the tick of time to sound once more.

CHAPTER 42

ARM AND HAMMER BEGAN THEIR FURIOUS journey downward toward the nail, but not before the returning angels carried their burdens into the bosom of the young carpenter.

The hammer smashed against the nail, and there were crucified in that instant

The first man, Adam
Adam's race
The fallen self
The wall of division between heathen and Jew
All governments
Principalities
Powers
Rule . . . and
Dominions.

Yes! *Crucified* upon the cross of our Lord Jesus Christ!

CHAPTER 43

ONCE MORE A NAIL WAS PRESSED DEEP into the other wrist. Once more the soldier drew his arm in a mighty upward swing, and once more the Lord froze time and eternity in their journey.

At that very instant one of the angels arrived at the base of Mount Sinai and began to sort furiously through the stones and rocks. He paused. There they lay, smashed, long forgotten. The stone tablets of the commandments and the law of Moses. Quickly the angel clutched them to his bosom, turned, and darted again for Jerusalem's holy Temple.

Arriving at the Temple courtyard, this same angel went straight into the Holy of Holies. Terrified, yet obedient, he lifted the mercy seat, reached inside the box of hammered gold, and brought forth the sacred copy of the law. He then gathered from within the Temple every rule, every regulation, every ordinance that ever had been penned, proclaimed, or dreamed of. *All* law, all legalism, all bondage!

The angel was about to depart when he heard again the Lord's voice within him. Turning, he called forth all ritual of all worship. Once more he would have departed, but turned again at the prodding of his glowing spirit. He now called forth all observance of all holy days. Finally he called forth even the Sabbath.

"You are but pictures of my Lord. Today pictures, types, and shadows of my Lord . . . end!"

At last he left the Temple, only to be stopped again. He breathed hard, turned, and called forth even the Temple!

"You, too. For even you are but a picture of my Lord. Today the picture ends!"

Now he rose high above the earth, and in a voice that reached all ends of all times, he commanded every rule, regulation, ritual, decree, and ordinance that had ever been observed by any religion ever practiced upon the face of the earth . . . to come forth!

Once more the burdened angel plunged downward through the skies, into time. He arrived just in time to lay his profound burden *into* the bosom of his Lord. He stepped back. "All this . . . ends . . . today!"

The hammer smashed against the nail. And with it,

All law
All rules
All ordinances
All holy days
And
All ritual

were crucified upon the cross of Jesus Christ our Lord!

CHAPTER 44

THE SOLDIERS BOUND THE LORD'S LEGS, pressed them hard against the wood, and nailed his feet to the cross. Ruthlessly they pulled the stake upward, balanced it, and then plunged it into a waiting hole. There was an awful thud and a pathetic groan.

Overhead the heavens were growing dark with some sick and mysterious cloud. Every moment the sky grew darker and more foreboding. Citizens of earth clutched their garments about them and shook inside at the sight of the foulness gathering in the sky above them.

What they saw were but small drops of vast, unholy things seeping through from unseen realms. The angels were now on the darkest and most dreadful of their journeys. Across time and space they flew, into every year, hour, and minute of human history. Into every village, town, and city. Across plain and desert, down even into the seas, they plunged. Rising, they brought back their dreadful cargo to Jerusalem, careful to stay in the invisibles, that they not drown earth with the very stench of their black wares. Darker and thicker grew the massive thing, as numberless angels wrestled to endure their burden until the appointed moment.

The Lord of earth grew faint upon his cross. His time was at an end.

With groans and wails and agonizing cries, the angels lifted their foul booty, stepped into time, and rushed up Golgotha's hill, carrying with them every sin of every man and woman who had ever lived!

Bringing together into one place this vile, pulsating, living thing called sin, they cast it *all* into the Lamb of God–who now became sin incarnate. All sin was now accumulated in one place–*in* him. Divinity now experienced that one thing it had never known. In the flood of that indescribably hideous invasion, the Lord of glory, forsaken of all holiness, cried out in delirium,

My God, my God,
Why hast thou forsaken me?

One of the archangels, blinded with rage and consumed with revenge, cried out savagely to his peers:

Now, now
to that place which is
the last moment of time.
Go, to our enemy! The prince of all princes!
Vengeance, vengeance!
Now, to the ends of wrath.
Vengeance, vengeance upon the damned one.
Go to that last moment
of creation.
Find him! Bring him to the cross!

Once more, to allow for the greatest of all retributions, time stood still.

CHAPTER 45

STREAKING THROUGH REALMS WHERE SPACE and time do not exist, the elect angels flew forward until they came to the ends of creation. And even there, angels found evidence of a cross. With swords raised and with eyes spewing fire, the angels stepped back into time, but a time which was the last second of the existence–in creation–of the kingdom of darkness.

It was Michael who cried out.

Vengeance!
Vengeance!
You–unholy equals–
meet your appointed hour!

Without pity, the elect angels whirled about the dark citizens of demondom–encircling them in fiery, blinding light–and drove them, screaming, back across eternity, back through the portal separating eternity from space-time. Out of the past, the dark host retreated, back toward Golgotha. The *final* moment of time was–at last–about to intersect with the centerpiece of the eternals. Demons of darkness looked up to see that cross, suspended outside creation, and knew by dark instinct they had a rendezvous with this instrument of destruction.

But when this rendezvous? In eternity past, or eternity future? The answer came suddenly enough.

Onward the elect angels mercilessly drove their gnashing, screaming, unholy prey, back toward the cross.

Two archangels with flashing, swirling swords hurled the dark fiends into the bosom of the only begotten Son of God, upon a cross that stood outside all dimensions.

Now went up a defiant cry from the angelic host as has never before–nor ever since–been heard. The whole host of angels and archangels swarmed *again*, into that mysterious portal to find somewhere, in some future place, that fiend of all fiends, and to finish with him a battle that began long ago at the throne of God.

"This time, victory!" they screamed, half mad with rage.

CHAPTER 46

IT WAS MICHAEL, inflamed with justice, who broke forth in that era that was the *final* moment of this age. There stood the prince of all principalities.

"Before you were created, you were defeated. In the eternals you were crucified on the cross of Christ. Now, damned foe, obey my words and go . . . or be driven . . . to that selfsame cross, in time and space!"

Lucifer snarled! But in a fury that matched the wrath of God, Michael drove the infernal angel back through all the ages, stumbling and screaming in full retreat. They stopped at the base of a hill. But not for long. The fire of Michael's unrelenting sword drove the dark prince toward the dying body of the *Lord* of all princes. There Lucifer found himself not only in time, but in a time he quickly recognized as Golgotha, the very place he had once believed to be the site of his greatest triumph! But no longer did he see the hill as he had seen it before. For an instant he saw the hill through eyes that see things as God sees them. What he beheld now was a cross upon which he had been crucified *before* creation!

By some unutterable means the fallen archangel was drawn inexorably into the very bosom of his enemy.

And so was crucified
The prince of darkness
and the
kingdom of darkness
upon the cross
of Jesus Christ, your Lord!

CHAPTER 47

WHILE TIME CONTINUED ITS REST, yet other elements of creation gave way to the all-destructive cross and plunged into the Son of God.

While angels watched in amazement, the entire world slipped out of time. That cross, now suspended in a vast realm of nothingness, drove time, space, matter, and eternity into its bosom. Both the visible and invisible creations, the entirety of the cosmological creation, began to melt into the bosom of the Crucified One, disappearing into the young man upon the cross. Time, eternity, and heavenly places soon vanished. The old creation–and all in it that has been diseased by the fall–had passed away!

The eyes of angels, viewing events from *outside* of time, watched as *all things* disappeared.

Before them now stood only a cross, hanging in a great void. All else was gone.

"We are seeing, for one glorious moment, that which the eyes of

God have always seen!" whispered the angel who bore the name Recorder.

Truly, he had kept his word. He had put away *all* death . . . *all things.*

Hallelujah!

CHAPTER 48

A COLD CHILL SWEPT OVER THE ANGELS. They had momentarily forgotten the one last and greatest enemy. That one with whom even they could do no battle.

Death now appeared out of nowhere! Even with creation crucified, the eternal cross had not yet faced that one who boasted of having no enemy except God. There were now only two beings remaining. One had claimed himself to be eternal life; the other claimed to be eternal death, and that by his hand life would die. Death, defiant and fearless, approached the cross and gurgled, in an obscene roar.

We meet again,
and now
for the last time!

Death stretched out his cloak and moved slowly toward his final prey.

The highest drama in universal history had begun!

Yes, Death,
*for the **last** time.*
Delay no longer. Come!

With that, the young carpenter once more moved his blood-soaked, iron-pierced hand. Creation suddenly reappeared. The scene returned to space and time. Earthly things once more came into view. Golgotha reappeared.

The Lord Jesus was now breathing his last breath. The angel of death moved inexorably on, covering the young carpenter with his seraphic wings. Death began squeezing the last breath of life from his final prey.

And Mary's son cried out with his last breath,

Father,
into
your hands
I commit
my Spirit.

With that, the carpenter died, soon to carry with him into the grave all enemies except one. Death, eternally dead, was still alive!

Death watched as life died, and then in a gesture of final victory he threw up his fist and shouted.

I have ended
*even **Life!***
***I** am victor*
and conqueror
of all things.

Death turned to go, darkness radiating from his face in a black, triumphant glow.

Out from somewhere, in a mystery beyond all knowledge, an immeasurable power laid hold of Death.

The black creature turned and screamed, "The Eternal Spirit!" Marshaling all his strength, he brought to bear upon this unseen power a force that caused the angels to drop to their knees in fear.

Angels, who had never dreamed that even one power so great existed, watched two such powers locked in final combat.

For a moment it seemed these powers were equal and that Death might wrest himself free. But slowly, relentlessly, the death angel was drawn toward the still, breathless figure hanging upon that wondrous tree. At last, his strength drained, Azell screamed in horror and disappeared into the bosom of the Nazarene.

And so were crucified *all* things. And such was the death of the Son of God.

Oh, yes.
There was one other thing
placed upon the cross
that day–
you were crucified with Christ.

PART 4

CHAPTER 49

"WE MUST HURRY, NICODEMUS. We have no more than an hour."

"But what of the girl? My servants say she is insisting that she be allowed to come here and prepare his body for burial."

"Impossible! It is now only a few minutes before the Sabbath begins. We hardly have time to purify ourselves before the holy day begins. And the girl, despite her devotion, should go and do likewise. It is not proper for her to be handling anything dead on the Sabbath."

"What should I tell her then? Already my servants have had to physically restrain her from coming to your garden."

"Tell her that she may come here on the day after Sabbath and *then* prepare his body for burial. I will instruct the gardener to unseal the tomb for her. But tell her she will need her friends, the other four women; it will be no small task."

Joseph of Arimathea motioned to his servants to begin the burial. They pulled back a huge slab of stone, revealing a very large tomb.

"It is a pity to put him into the tomb . . . this way. It is not a pretty sight."

"But you have allowed him a good place to be buried," replied Nicodemus. "It is a beautiful garden, and only fitting for such a prophet as he to be planted in the ground in such a verdant setting."

At that moment, unseen by any earthly eye, no less than an archangel strolled into the garden and knelt beside the cold, still form of the Son of God. He stared at his side and a wound made by a Roman spear. "Yes," whispered the angel. "Exactly the same place. A gaping hole. And something missing! Only this time *not* a bone!"

The servants surrounded the body of the Nazarene and carefully placed him in the ground . . . as one might plant a lonely, solitary seed.

With that the two men departed the garden, leaving a leaderless archangel to contemplate the scene before him.

"An open side. A singular species . . . one who died without ever knowing a counterpart . . . now cold and still. This lonely one who abode alone for so long . . . has ceased to exist. And now . . . now he is planted in the soil . . . as a *seed*? The earth has become a grave for the Seed of all seeds.

"And what a grave it is. God is buried there! Does no one realize, *God* is buried here! Never has there been such a grave. Buried with him, principalities, powers, all darkness, the enmity between Jew and heathen, Adam . . . sin . . . all creation! And . . . oh yes . . . one small comfort–Death . . . *he* lies also here entombed!

"No, never has there been such a grave.

"*We* shall wait out our time here," resolved the archangel.

"Out of a scene quite like this, in another garden, came forth a bride for Adam. Kind of his kind.

"Sons of God? Is such a thing possible? *Sons of God? Daughters of God?* Like unto his like? Kind of *his* kind?

"A *counterpart* to our Lord?

"But how?

"It may be–though I know not by what means–this matter shall be concluded *here*, in a fashion worthy of a God who, when he was alive, was ever a bit mysterious and quite prone to the unexpected."

CHAPTER 50

SHE AWOKE WITH A START. It was that dream again. *Dawn will soon be here,* she thought. *Then I can cease this pretense of sleep.*

Over and over again, in her dreams, she watched him crucified. She was weary and desperate for sleep, but always, the same dream . . . Golgotha!

But *something* in that dream was amiss.

His *side*!

She sat upright.

That was it. His side. The soldier had pierced his side at the moment of his death. She had seen it and screamed in terror. Now she recalled: From the open wound had poured forth blood and water.

"That simply is not possible!" she murmured. "What does it mean?"

She dropped her head and began once more to pour out copious tears from already swollen eyes . . . and wondered how long until the appointed dawn. She lay back down and for a moment drifted off to sleep, only to wake with a cry. It was that dream again.

She would wait no longer. She would go now to the tomb, while it was still night. The others would know to meet her there. At his grave she might find solace and perhaps even sleep. She slipped out of her bed and reached for the basket filled with jars and vases that she had so carefully prepared the evening before.

A few moments later the young girl stepped out into the dark of Jerusalem's streets, carrying with her the precious aloes, oils, spices, and ointments she would use in preparing her Lord for proper burial. She shuddered to recall that men had callously placed his body into the earth so hastily.

The watchman hesitated only an instant before opening the gate to allow the young girl to depart the city. She paused in the darkness. Her eyes could penetrate the night for only a few feet.

"The hill is in that direction," she said to herself, "as is Joseph's house. And beyond that, the garden."

I worshiped him, I loved him, when he lived, she thought. *He is dead now; but alive or dead, it makes no difference: he is my Lord.*

Down the road she went, then across a meadow to a narrow pathway. Leaving that, she mounted a steep, grassy hill.

Suddenly the earth beneath her feet quivered, jolted, and then shook with a violence. The very planet seemed to be shuddering in the presence of some catastrophic power.

The young girl was flung to the ground. Her basket and its contents were scattered everywhere. She buried her fingers into the grass and held on with all her might. A deep tremble seemed to be coming from the very bowels of the earth, increasing in force as it neared the surface.

Bursting forth at last, the tremor twisted the earth savagely. Chimneys began to fall, roads cracked, and graves split open. The crust of the earth began to roll like an ocean wave. Then came a deafening crack, followed, hard on, by a burst of light. In the midst of this chaotic display of unbridled power, the first small gleam of day made its appearance.

Sunday morning was in the throes of birth.

CHAPTER 51

THE TOMB WAS NOT SPARED the onslaught of this strange earthquake, for it, too, reeled in violence. The tomb was, in fact, the epicenter of the quake. No. Not the tomb, but the corpse. Some unearthly power, it seems, had stolen inside that bloodstained body.

All the powers of the Eternal Spirit had met *in* him, there to engage Death in the most titanic struggle of all the ages.

The concentration of energy spiraled, the force of the conflict intensified. Death had died upon the cross, true, but all its powers had frozen an eternal grip upon the soul of its last victim. Earth's foundations trembled in the presence of this struggle to loose Death's unbreakable grip. Creation itself shuddered under the strain while earth released a deep groan, crying out for its redemption. The body of the carpenter reverberated. This Power, whatever it was, was building. The tomb cracked, moaned, and reeled.

For one fleeting instant a soft glow appeared in the tomb, its origin *inside* the lifeless body . . . a momentary foregleam of some enormous force inside him struggling to the surface. One of the carpenter's hands jerked at the upward surge of power from within. There was a burst of light–a light so intense it struck blind the entire heavenly host awaiting without.

All the power and light of eternity had accumulated in one soul and then exploded from out of the bosom of the Son of God–the grave, the earth, the skies, the angels dazzled in a reflected light. For one instant it seemed creation might well dissolve ere the light abated.

The carpenter's body was now engulfed in the purity and holiness of this light. His corpse seemed to disappear in a furnace of liquid radiance. Or had it only *changed*?

Eternal Life had poured out the total content of its power and, in the midst of that explosion, the *form* of flesh had been swallowed up by an eternal and deathless body. A body as spiritual as the Spirit was now blazing from within him!

Now came a thunderous shout . . . from within the tomb!

"I am alive!"

Instantly, without thought or instinct, this man rising out of the sleep of death–like the first man Adam had done before him–grabbed his side.

"A scar! A scar on my side!

"Something is *missing* from *me*! Something . . . someone . . . that has been inside me for all eternity is now missing!"

He rose up *through* the grave cloth, sprang to his feet, and flung off the headpiece.

"Divisible! I have become divisible.

"She who was hidden *in* me for all eternity . . . she has come forth from my side.

"Bone of my bone . . . flesh of . . .

"Nay!" he roared. "Spirit of my Spirit, life of my Life . . . essence of my Essence," he exclaimed, raising both arms high above his head in exultation.

It is true, you see, that if one should thrust his hand into the earth, he will surely bring forth earth. And if one should thrust his hand into the side of man, he will surely bring forth humanity. And, perchance, should one thrust his hand into the side of God, he will surely bring forth divinity!

Something of God had come forth from God, just as surely as something of Adam had come forth from Adam. As Eve was the substance of Adam, so was someone, somewhere, the substance of *him.*

Ironic, is it not, that the singular, most perfect creature in all the universe–standing there in a translated body radiating all the light of the glory of God–had upon his side . . . *a scar*! The evidence of the price he had paid for a counterpart.

Now he raised his hands and face in triumph, and roared, "Where are my rivals? Where are my enemies?"

As was the seed,
so was I,
alone.

Into the earth
I fell
and died.
As did the seed,
so did I.
The Seed
has risen–
I am now risen
and am no more
alone.

First, but
a vision
hidden in
my heart,

now, out of this grave,
my counterpart!

He roared again,

"Her suitors and enemies? Where are her enemies? The damnation that infested the creation . . . where is it?"

The brightness of God billowed forth from him as cataracts of torrential light. For one instant he stood, not in a tomb, nor on earth, but outside the boundaries of eternity . . . God . . . an eternal man . . . crucified . . . risen . . . triumphant over all things.

He cried out in a voice that reached across the boundaries of all creation,

All things are under my feet!
I am RISEN!
Alive forevermore
I am risen from the grave.
Hallelujah!

CHAPTER 52

HE TURNED AND WALKED THROUGH the stone slab; for though his body was still physical, the *physical* of *this* man now belonged to the *spirituals*!

The assembled host of heaven had for three days awaited him. In the garden, upon the hills, round about Jerusalem, as far as unseen eyes could see, the innumerable citizenry of the other realm had waited.

As he stepped forth through the rock, a dazzling fire of liquid light engulfing him, the legions of elect angels broke forth in a wild delirium of praise.

Some of the angels soared, others knelt, most shouted, a few simply flailed their arms. A smaller number jumped up and down. It is even reported–though not confirmed–that some hugged one another, and danced about most unangelically.

One of the archangels, then another, rose into the air and arched about the throng in an enormous circle, leaving a trail of sparkling light in their flight. Soon the entire host joined in this heavenly display, circling about the risen Lord, a veritable tornado of whirling light.

The Lord over Death signaled to the two archangels. Quickly they came and rolled back the door of the tomb, revealing, for all eyes to see, the emptiest tomb on all the face of the earth.

Once more, angels quite beside themselves with joy turned jubilation into chaotic praise.

The Lord signaled for silence, and though they were never so willing to obey him as now, the praise would begin to subside only to soar again, boiling over to new heights of thunderous adoration. At last the heavenly host fell silent.

A look of defiance had been steadily growing upon the face of the Lord, a thing that seemed somehow almost inappropriate for such a moment. He turned and looked back at the empty tomb, his eyes blazing with the brightness of a thousand infernos.

The Lord lifted his hand again. At some silent command of its Creator, the garden began to fade, as did hills and valleys, sky and stars. All creation seemed to evaporate. Suspended in a vast realm of nothing, there was now nothing present. Nothing save the angels, their Lord, and a tomb.

Every angel knew they were *not* at Jerusalem, nor were they in time. The angels stood, they were certain, either at a time before creation or in some far-future age that would exist after this creation had disappeared and been forgotten.

What is it I see? wondered Michael.

The cross, unbound by creation, existed before creation, in creation, and beyond creation? It is eternal! So also is the emptiness of the tomb and the triumphant resurrection of our Lord. What does this mean? What is the fate of those things crucified with him, for they were crucified outside of and beyond the effects of time.

Michael knew he would soon have his answer, for his Lord was about to speak.

I have risen from you, O grave.
Now, world, with all your glitter,
you were buried with me.
Now, of your own power, come forth!

There followed the thunder of silence.
Once again he spoke.

Principalities, powers, rulers, and dominions–
you who held sway over man
and held him captive to your system,
you who boasted and flaunted that power–
you were crucified with me!
Now if you can, come forth!

Regal silence reigned.

Prince of darkness–you who
vied for my throne,
you who would have ruled creation,
here, in the eternals,
I declare to you
that which you do not yet know in time:
you were placed in my bosom
and shared this tomb with me–
now of your own vaunted authority, come forth!

Silence fairly screamed in reply.

Now the Lord roared with a passion that unnerved the heartiest angel.

Death–you, the final victor
in all earth's dramas,
you, with a power unrelenting–

by that vaunted power,
greater than all others combined,
Death,
of your own power
live!
Death–damned Death–by
your power,
RISE!

A moment of unbearable silence ensued, while angelic eyes strained to see what would come of such defiance.

Nothing moved!

"Know then, Azell, angel of death, you have died! One day, in time, you shall rue the hour you came for my life. When you approached my cross, you have swept your sickle across the ages of men, where you harvested with your blade! Creation and all in it have vanished forever. By my cross and by this tomb you have passed away."

Grave . . . where is your victory,
Death, where is your sting?

Creation and all in it had truly vanished forever, vanquished by a cross and a tomb.

The Lord and angels broke forth in spontaneous chorus. Surely the angels would have done themselves harm if they had not given vent to the praise that was welling up from within them . . . except that the Lord brought them to stunned silence as he declared:

"And now, at long last, I will reveal to you–from ages unknown–the *Mystery* hidden in God!"

CHAPTER 53

THE MYSTERY! There were angelic legends of such a thing. The angel Recorder had whispered of it. But none knew of its meaning nor its content.

A mystery utterly hidden, for it was hidden *in* God.

Once again the Lord raised his right hand.

A great rend appeared in the fabric of the nothingness that surrounded them. What the angels saw within the strange portal was *time* . . . moving *backward.* There was Moses, then Noah, Adam's tragic fall, the creation of man, the creation of earth and stars.

Then rose before their eyes a backward chronicle of eternity–the creation of the angels, an event they all remembered, for it was the *first* of all their memories. Then back to the creation of the *first* angel, Recorder. Then that moment when a limitless God enfolded himself and entered eternity. And then in the backward flight of universal history . . . even eternity ended!

The angels watched spellbound as a scene appeared before them that antedated even eternity's dawn.

They beheld–for the first time–God in his unlimited state. God, the All, *before* all things! Not even in the wildest imagining of their spirits could they have conceived of a God so utterly without limit, so vast, so powerful, so all-encompassing. They were seeing their Lord God *before* he enfolded himself and entered that small realm called eternity. They were seeing God as he *really* is! Some dropped to their knees; others, knowing not what to do, covered their eyes in the presence of such revealed glory.

Somehow, this incredible vision was beginning to change. The angelic host was being allowed to see *the very center* of God.

The idea of a mystery had momentarily slipped from them. But now the purpose of this unveiled vision came to them with stunning suddenness. They were peering into the very center of the depths of God. Yet not one among them could conceive of what mystery lay hidden there.

The scene before them grew brighter; great shafts of sparkling light and storms of flashing brightness emerged. Then, at the very core of this ocean of Godness, *marked-off* portions of his being began to become evident. And move.

Something was there . . . hidden in the very center of God.

Somehow the angels grasped that they were seeing that very instant, far back in that pre-eternal age, when their Lord was marking off portions of his being for some high and future purpose. Portions of his being, destined . . . *before* the foundation of the ages . . . for what? They waited. The *marked-off* portions of God soon numbered in the millions.

The scene was, somehow, changing again! Every angel felt as if he were seeing something familiar, yet he knew not what! Those marked-off portions of God were glistening like . . . an indescribably beautiful . . . what? A city?

"I thought for a moment I saw a city! For certain, a form of some kind is emerging from the brightness of the light."

That *something* was becoming a *someone*!

One startled angel, comprehending the first hint of what was gradually forming before their eyes, cried out in shocked amazement.

"Jeru!"

The form continued changing, coming into ever-sharper focus.

Throughout the angelic body could be heard repeated again and again, "Not Jeru, at all, but Eve. Eve . . . it is Eve."

Still the form grew in beauty and in glory. Ten thousand times ten thousand angels fell to their knees, struck down as one, by beauty alone.

There were cries of glory, shouts not unlike sobs, and unprecedented weeping. Some covered their faces, while others raised their hands in exultation.

"More than Eve! Far more than Eve!"

Every angel was now remembering that unforgettable moment when, during the creation of Eve, the glory of God overwhelmed all creation. It was a thing that, until now, they had never understood. Now they knew! When the Lord created Eve, he was "seeing" *someone* else. He had fashioned Eve in the image of an exotically beautiful woman who belonged to some other dimension.

That woman now stood before them. There was no question, Eve was but the foreshadowing of *this one.* Before them stood a woman of incomparable glory and beauty, made up of unnumbered millions of portions of God's own being–portions of God chosen, before the foundation of the ages, to be the composites of her being.

Here, at last, was the Mystery *who* had been hidden in God!

Angels hardly dared to look upon such terrible beauty, yet they dared not do otherwise.

Here was a woman, robed in the very brightness and glory of God, with a beauty defying their comprehension. She was like *him*, yet female! A loveliness so tender, a countenance so full of love, a being so pure that angelic eyes shone with awe and terror seeking to take it in. She had been formed out of God. She did not belong to creation, for he is uncreated. And, as Eve was bone of Adam's bone, this woman was spirit of the Lord's Spirit. The uncreated God had revealed to them his counterpart. A woman fashioned out of the water and spirit of an uncreated God, being of his being.

Her hair was black as ravens, her youth had once inspired a creating God to fashion springtime. Her features encompassed all the beauty of every race and tribe and kindred of womanhood from all ends of creation, for each of them had been but a portion, a picture, of her.

Mercifully, the vision of the glorious woman began to recede. Once more there appeared before the angels the scene of the *All* of God. Exhausted, angels fell prostrate upon their faces.

"No suitors, no rivals, no enemies," one whispered.

"The mother of Eve," responded another.

"A new Jeru," declared yet another in soft delirium.

One of the angels stood, still half-blinded by glory, and uttered, "A counterpart for our Lord!"

"The bride of God!"

"We saw her for but a moment. When will this woman, not formed of things created, not belonging to the fallen creation of the old heaven and the old earth . . . when shall she fully appear before us?"

The answer was evident to all. When the last scene of an already crucified cosmos passed in its forward journey through space and time and the last tick sounded in the continuum of time, when absolutely all that God created in those six days of creation had forever vanished, *then* would this girl, *who* is the *new* creation . . . then would she appear before them.

"Then," whispered one of the archangels, "when there is nothing but the new creation, made up only of things uncreated . . . *then* there will be a wedding!"

CHAPTER 54

WHILE STILL INTOXICATED BY GLORY, the angels began to stagger to their feet. Not one would have dreamed there was yet more to this unveiling.

The resurrected Lord moved toward this pre-eternal scene that he had unveiled before his angels by means of a rend in the fabric of creation. At the same moment the vision of the All of God, out there in pre-eternity, seemed to be moving *toward* the carpenter!

That endless sea of God now poised at the edge of the portal they had been peering into. It seemed the All of God was about to pour out of past eternity into time and space. The Lord Jesus, in turn, moved closer to the portal . . . paused, then raised his hand. That limitless divinity, seen, until now, only as a vision, broke through the Door separating the two ages and began pouring into the visible realm, into time, into space!

The angels gasped.

The All of God was flowing out of that age which was *before* the ages and was pouring *into* the Son of God! The angels, one and all, considered shielding their eyes, but one and all decided to choose blindness over missing the sight of this awesome phenomenon.

The Lord Jesus began to glow, his brightness *in this realm* growing until it matched the brightness of the All of God in that age before the eternals. Could the All of God–unlimited–be contained inside the body of a *man*? Such a thought was beyond angelic imagination! Yet, he was, after all, a resurrected Lord–abiding in a translated body.

The scene became more incredible as the ends of a now endless God continued sweeping into the Lord of lords.

Still the infusion continued until the *very center* of a pre-eternal God came once more into view. The *center* of the All of God began to pour into the Nazarene! Now even those portions of God–marked off in him before the foundation of the ages–began to move toward Christ Jesus. The mystery was about to pour into the Nazarene. The mystery was about to be hidden in *him*! The Lord lifted his hand once more. The forward flow of divine life paused. By some amazing power, the carpenter reached forth through the Door and drew into his hand the very *first* portion of divinity that had been marked off in God so long ago! Plucking this light of Life, he held it high in his hand for the angels to see. It glistened like diamond fire.

Once again the totality of the All of God resumed its plunge into the bosom of the Son of God. The forward flow came to an end. The All of God was now in Christ Jesus. That which was marked off in God before creation's foundation was now in him. That woman was now *in* him as ever she had been.

Suddenly the angels realized this vision had been allowed them so that they might understand the riches that had always been hidden in Christ Jesus. For one dazzling instant the brightness of the All of God shone forth–a torrent of living light–from *within* the Nazarene. The brightness was too intense, too exquisite for any eyes to see fully. Angels, eyes drowned in glory, reached out their hands trying to sense what their blinded eyes could no longer see.

Gradually the light began to fade from their view, as it slipped yet deeper inside the Son of God. At last the glory in angelic eyes began to recede. They could see again.

The Lord of all this glory stood there, alone. He was holding in his hand that *first* dazzlingly bright portion of marked-off divinity. Every angel of heaven knew *that* portion of God had been destined for some incredibly special purpose.

In their seeing of this imponderable vision, they had beheld eternity past and eternity future. As it had been three days before, they had been allowed to see things–such as their enemy, the prince of all principalities–crucified. Now they would have to return to space-time. But in the same moment they were certain that their God–the I AM–remained free of *their* limitation. To him the dissolution of the fallen creation, and all that was in it–had already taken place. They were looking at a Lord who was even at that moment *in* the new creation and who was viewing all things from that vantage point!

Each angel sighed a sigh of disappointment. They were about to return to that lesser place where reality was not so easy to see. They were returning to the confines of space-time. The tomb, which had dissolved from view when this vision commenced, now gradually began to reappear. The hills round about Jerusalem came once more into view. The morning sun was shining brightly in the sky.

While they had been peering into that age past, a few minutes of time had been allowed to pass there in the garden. Every eye of every angel fixed itself on that brightly burning element of divinity the Lord still held high in his hand.

Why was he doing this? Surely the very end of the Mystery was about to be known.

CHAPTER 55

"WE ARE BACK IN TIME AND SPACE," declared one of the angels. "Yet that woman we saw . . . do you realize that even as we stand in this temporal creation, *she* is *in* him?"

"Yes, and he–like Adam–now has an open side from which can come his . . . counterpart . . . into time, into space!"

"Is that possible?" interrupted another. "We stand in the old, fallen creation. The new creation has not begun."

"Do not be certain," chimed in another. "I remind you of what you witnessed upon the cross and at the tomb. *That* creation has been put away! In *his* eyes, from where *he* stands, it is over."

"So, be certain of nothing when speaking of *his* way," interrupted yet another angel. "And besides, unless I have missed it all, *she* is the new creation!"

"Attention, now, for he speaks again!"

In the most formal and human of ways the young carpenter mounted a stone near the center of the garden and motioned for silence. The bright, glowing portion of divinity was still in his hand and was being held above his head.

"Long ago I declared that I would never create again. But upon my cross that creation, that *old* creation of which I spoke . . . *passed away*!

"I shall now fashion a *new* creation! I shall begin that new creation here. My new creation is beyond the tomb and is *one* with my resurrection . . . *now*!"

What news this was for an angelic host–long saddened by daily watching a creation that had gone so completely astray from its original intention. This was, in fact, what they would, from this day forward, refer to as "the good news."

A grand "Hallelujah" rolled across the heavenly assemblage.

"But when I speak of creating a new creation, imagine not orbiting planets, endless galaxies, nor even heavenly realms! *That* was the *old*. The inauguration of my new creation will be none of those. Nor shall I create a thing *material*; nor shall I even create anything spiritual.

"I shall not *create* at all."

Revelation swept across the faces of the angels. The Lord's words (unlike his ways) were rarely mysterious.

"I shall not create at *all*. I shall *build*. I shall fashion . . . out of my own being the many parts of my new creation. One day I shall assemble these parts into one whole. But I *cannot* create the new creation. This new thing that I began this day is composed of that which is uncreated!

"The firstfruits of my new creation shall be built out of my *own* nature! My essence. My being. My *life*. The first of my new creation shall be built out of *me*! As I formed Eve out of Adam's flesh . . . as I built her out of Adam's bone . . . even so shall I form the new creation out of my own Spirit. I shall build the new creation out of my very being."

A murmur of awe rippled across the angels. The riddle, at last, was solved.

"As I built Eve out of the bone of Adam, bone of his bone, flesh of his flesh, so shall I build my counterpart . . . spirit of my Spirit . . . life of my Life.

"This woman shall be composed of many portions of my being. Not in one hour, nor even in one day, shall I form her. But today I will *begin.*"

"*Another* mystery," thought the angels.

"As surely as I rose *this day* from the grave . . . so she also shall rise–this day–from that selfsame grave. She was in me, and today she rose from the grave . . . with me! Today, in the presence of an open tomb . . . today, the day of my resurrection, marks the *beginning* of that new creation!

"Now look to the tomb!

"From out of that tomb shall come the very *firstfruit* of that creation. Today, I *commence* the greatest of all deeds. Today I *begin* the creation, nay, the *building* . . . of my bride! What you are about to see is but a faint miniature of what I will continue to do until the completion of time. I will build a new creation even in the presence of the dissolution of the old, to demonstrate my manifold wisdom and to shame my enemy!"

The angelic assembly found themselves in a state of pure confusion, compounded with elation.

"Look to the tomb!" cried the Lord, holding high the portion of *life* within his hand.

Not until they turned to look at the tomb did they realize, in amazement, that something–no, *someone*–was *in* that tomb.

CHAPTER 56

GRADUALLY THE EARTHQUAKE BEGAN TO SUBSIDE. The frightened young girl raised her head. All around her was evidence of a violent upheaval; even the ground where she lay was rent with fissures. Rising to her knees, she began to gather up the precious ointments that were scattered about.

Fear, doubt, and wonder gripped her heart as she rose and began walking toward the garden. Her footsteps slowed. A strange and powerful foreboding descended on her. For a moment she simply stood, staring transfixed at the garden entrance. Closing her eyes, she pushed open the door. Slowly she moved toward his tomb, dread in every step. There, in the semidarkness of morning, she spied the open tomb.

"Oh no!" she cried. "They have taken him. They have taken the body of my Lord! It is gone. It is gone!"

For a moment the young girl could only stand in horror. Then she turned and began running, crying all the while, "Peter! I must tell Peter! Surely I can find Peter. He hides, I know not where. But I will find him. He will know what to do."

And surely she did find Peter, hiding with another of the disciples. To them she reported her wild story.

They would go and see this incredible thing.

At the garden door, John broke into a run. Peter ran after him. Arriving at the tomb's entrance, John stood there, dazed. Peter pulled him aside and went in. A moment later he staggered out, more insensible even than John.

"Please, please, I know the danger, Peter, but you must go to the authorities. You must find out where they have taken my Lord's body."

"My life may be the forfeit, but I *will* find out," replied Peter soberly.

The three turned from the tomb, their destination,the authorities. But after a few steps the young girl turned.

"No, I will stay. Perhaps Joseph or one of his servants–perhaps the keeper of the garden . . . someone–will return here. If I have news I will come to you. If you have news, *please* send someone to me."

Peter nodded. "Whatever you wish. Follow your heart, as, toward him, you always did."

The young girl returned to the tomb. She knelt at its entrance and, motionless, stared inside.

A strange desire began to grow in her heart . . . the desire to go *into* the tomb. Cautiously she moved through the door and took in the scene: the shroud, the head cover, the very place where he had lain. She was overcome. The young girl fell to her knees and began to weep. Tears of sorrow, cries of agony rose from a shattered heart. On and on, quite uncontrollably she wept, until at last, merciful sleep fell upon her.

It was a sleep so deep it seemed akin to death.

Who is this amazing young girl?

CHAPTER 57

THE ANGELS WERE IN TOTAL CONFUSION.

Someone was in that tomb. The resurrected Lord had come forth from that tomb; nothing else had. All else had been put away. Had something, or someone, broken free of the destructive power of the cross?

No, that was impossible. Nonetheless, someone was *in* that tomb! And whoever it was, of this they were certain–that *someone* was quite dead!

The Lord spoke.

"I will show you now the firstfruit of my salvation. I will show you the beginnings of my new creation. I will show you . . ." His voice wavered. ". . . the first *portion* of my counterpart."

"And one day, when the last portion of my being–marked off and predestined before the world's foundation–when *that* last portion of my being has been implanted into the very last person destined to be redeemed . . . then shall there be an assembling. Outside of time, beyond the end of this creation, the assembling together . . . and then . . . oh . . . then!"

But who was in that tomb? This was the question burning in the spirit of every angel. A bride . . . made up of many portions? Or just a portion of the bride? What could be this "new creation"? An entire creation made up only of the substance and being of God? Had they understood him?

It all seemed quite impossible, especially in the light of the extreme and dire condition of fallen mankind. Yet they had seen *this* creation annihilated. What would take its place?

Their answers, they knew, would soon be forthcoming, because . . . whoever was in that tomb . . . had just stirred!

It was a girl. A young girl. Once a terrible sinner–yes, the worst of the whole lot. And, from within the tomb, *she* was moving toward the open door. She was coming out of the tomb, a harbinger of things unseen.

The Lord held yet higher that portion of his own being, making sure that every angel eye could see. His hand began to move. They stood mesmerized as he placed that bright portion of his being into his wounded side.

His side now glistened in splendrous glory.

The young girl had come almost to the very entrance of the tomb. Her eyes were filled with tears; the light of the morning sun was in her face.

"Gardener?" she said.

The angels stood frozen in anticipation.

CHAPTER 58

"GARDENER?" SHE SAID AGAIN. She began to wipe her eyes with her cloak and tried hard to peer past the morning's bright sun.

"Where have you taken my Lord's body? Please tell me, and I will go to him and care for him."

She now stood on the very threshold of the tomb's doorway. By now, every angel knew this girl was a symbol of what had happened and what would continue to take place as a result of the resurrection. If the Lord's words had not been misunderstood, *whoever* comes forth from the resurrection of their Lord, that person belongs to the *next* creation and has nothing to do with *this* creation. In another instant that former sinner would step forth out of the grave.

The Lord raised his hand. The angels knew that sight. They expected time, once more, to stand still. But it did not. On this occasion it only *slowed.*

The Lord motioned to his angels to look toward the girl. They gasped. Their Lord was allowing them to see right into her heart.

There, deep inside her, they could see that still, gray thing, that which had once been the very glory and center of Adam. They could see the human spirit of this girl lying dead. The human spirit, dead since the fall of Adam . . . no longer able to function toward the unseen realm . . . the very realm from which it had originally come.

Suddenly, the angels realized! This was the Lord *over* death who stood before them. If *he* had risen from the dead, he was himself the power to *raise* the dead. He *was* Resurrection. *He* could bring to life things dead. Yea, he could even resurrect the human spirit–and make it live again! After all these millenia, could the human spirit . . . live? Again? For the first time that morning they really *believed* he might do all the astounding things he said he would do!

"Eve was *in* Adam," said one of the archangels softly, to give utterance to the thoughts of them all.

The Lord calmly lowered his hand and began to reach toward his wounded side . . . to bring forth something out of his side that was *in* him . . . and *of* him. A portion of that Mystery, of that woman who was inside God, was about to be loosed in time and space. A portion of God was about to be . . .

The archangel, now grasping what was about to happen, spoke again.

"Eve came forth from Adam's side."

The Lord drew forth from *within* his side the very Life of God, blazing in light. He proceeded to cast this very portion of his own Life toward the girl. Yet as he did, by mysteries beyond knowing, the stream of light and Life remained flowing from his bosom, unbroken.

Slowly, the luminous ball of fiery Life approached the girl, making her glow within its radiant glory. Just as that light of Life was about to make flight into her heart, the human spirit–long since dead–ignited into glorious life.

The human spirit *had* risen from the dead!

A shout of joy rose from the angels . . . only to subside quickly in wonder.

The archangel spoke again.

"Eve was bone of Adam's bone. This one shall be spirit of our Lord's Spirit."

Still they could not believe their eyes.

The human spirit, made alive by the divine Spirit, was now melting . . . becoming part of the Lord's own spirit. That Spirit–that Life–now moved *inside* the young girl!

"Essence of his Essence," continued the angelic recitation, as the resurrected spirit within the girl, and the divine Spirit from within him . . . became *one.*

The angels were now beholding grace beyond all bounds of imagination as two spirits melted together into one.

"Eve was joined to Adam and the two became . . . one flesh."

The Spirit of the Life of the Lord had now entered into the young girl! Her whole internal being was ablaze with the light of the glory of God. The Life of God was in her, and *one* with her! The angels were forced to shield their eyes once more. And the minds of their spirits were filled as much with glory as were their eyes. She had been *in him* before earth's foundation–*now* he was in her.

The two shared *one* Spirit.

The resurrected Lord had become *the indwelling Christ!*

Once more, who is this girl?

CHAPTER 59

"SUCH GLORY," MURMURED GABRIEL TO HIMSELF.

"The spirit of man alive again. What glory!

"The soul redeemed, and now being transformed into the spirituals. What glory!"

His eyes saddened.

"But the body . . . still fallen. Still so utterly fallen. That poor tragic body of fallen–and redeemed–man. For that body, is there no hope of glory?"

Suddenly Gabriel caught sight of yet something else, something that had been implanted within the young girl.

Gabriel saw *inside* that ball of blazing Life that had just entered the girl, something tiny beyond all infinitesimal measure. Gabriel was now gazing at a *seed*! No! More than a seed. For he could see even *inside* that seed! *Within* that seed . . . waiting for some moment when it would be called forth . . . was a translated body. A body not too unlike the translated body of the resurrected Lord. A body wholly physical, yet wholly spiritual, now encased in an infinitesimally small seed . . . inside the Life of God . . . which was now inside the girl.

Gabriel knew somehow, intuitively, that the seed of that body would remain hidden–and forgotten–inside the bosom of the girl . . . until . . . until when?

"Until," Gabriel spoke only to himself, "until I call forth that seed with the sound of a mighty trumpet . . . with the trump of God. In *that* day, the *last* day, a spiritual body shall burst forth out of that seed . . . burst out and swallow up her present body . . . and mortality shall put on immortality.

"Yes, even for the body, there is *the hope of glory*!"

Gabriel strained to hold his being in control as this thought now overwhelmed him.

Others of the angels were struck dumb when, suddenly, they heard Gabriel, almost beside himself, shout with a shout that almost ruptured the earth.

"Behold, full salvation!

"Behold, the new creation!"

Every eye turned again toward the girl.

She stood in the door of the tomb, covered in a brightness of light not seen since creation. The very purity of God radiated from her like rivers of living fire.

The spirit was alive. Divine Life was in her. Her own spirit was one with his. In it all, the soul had been washed as white as snow and was, even now, being transformed by the Spirit of the divine Life radiating out of the spirit into her soul.

"Behold!" thundered Gabriel. "A human being has become partaker of the divine Life."

"Behold," he cried again, as only Gabriel could, "standing before you that which has never been before. A new species. *A new creation!*

"Behold *the new creation.* Being of his Being. Essence of his Essence. Life of his Life.

"A new creation, *in* Christ Jesus!"

Pure, exquisite bedlam would have broken out at this point, except that the angels realized the beautiful woman who had stepped out of the tomb–dimming all other lights–was about to speak.

In a moment the Lord would lift his hand again, and time would resume its quicker pace, and eyes would again see only the dull things that those with physical eyes are given to see. But at this moment a woman of breathtaking beauty, robed in the purity, righteousness, holiness–and light–of God, had stepped forth from the tomb.

What did the Lord see in that moment?

A girl. A bride! Young. Spotless. Created, nay, built out of the Godness of God. In *his* eyes, she was perfect. And, in his eyes, all *his* rivals–and all her enemies and suitors–no longer existed.

For one bright moment, *through his eyes*, he saw them as . . . the only two living things. Through *his* eyes he saw her somewhere out in post-eternity standing before him, perfect and complete, the divine love of God beating passionately in her–and that same love beating in him. The triumphant Lord and his counterpart! A glorious bride without spot or wrinkle, washed in the blood of the Lamb.

Through *his* eyes he saw a girl who, like him, had risen from the tomb, beyond death's reach, beyond the reaches of all imperfection. She . . . risen, triumphant over the grave. Death beneath her feet.

This is what his eyes saw. *What other eyes may see is of no matter.*

Who is this incredible girl? Do you not yet know?

You are that girl!

CHAPTER 60

"RABBONI! OH, DEAR TEACHER!"

She lunged toward him with an abandon that defied all description. And having reached him she clutched him with all her might.

Up until now she had loved him with all her mind, her soul, and her heart. That is, she had loved him with all her human nature. But now, for the first time, she was also loving him–passionately–with all her spirit! For the first time, the Lord of glory was being loved with the *divine* drive of *the love of God*, a love that, until now, was found only in him.

It was quite obvious to everyone, too, that this young girl fully intended never to let him go.

With a warm laugh he said, "Little one, you must release your hold on me; I must ascend . . . to my Father.

"Now go. Go to my brothers. Tell them–

I am ascending to my Father

and ***your*** *Father,*
to my God
and your God."

"But Lord, if I depart this place . . . and if you ascend, then I will never see you again," she replied.

"Little one, little one. Be assured. For now . . . and for all ages, I will not–I cannot–*ever* leave you."

The young girl, her eyes filled with tears, her heart bursting with joy, dropped to the ground and kissed his feet.

A moment later this young girl, who had known only to love him and adore him, left the garden to declare a word she knew full well would never be believed.

The angels watched her depart and whispered among themselves.

"She is not his counterpart, is she?"

"No," was the assured reply.

"Yet, yes!" came an answer just as assured. "She is part of–the *first* part of–his bride."

"His bride, it is so clear now, will be made up of *all* the redeemed."

"But how is that possible?"

"That I know not, but after these three days, are you willing to say it is *not* possible?"

"Did you see?" observed another excitedly.

"See what?"

"I am sure of it. You recall the vision? Remember, for one brief instant, he allowed us to look into eternity past (or was it eternity future?) and see his completed bride. She was beautiful beyond all telling. But did you not see! The young girl . . . as she stepped forth from the tomb . . . her features . . . something of that young girl's features was there in the features of the bride of Christ. I am certain of it."

"That," said another, "is because that young girl is *part of* that bride."

"The wonder of it all!" said yet another angel as he shook his head, almost, but not quite, in disbelief.

"Do you not realize," muttered yet one more angel, in total awe, "do you not realize, his bride has never even *seen* the old creation. She belongs to an age beyond the fallen cosmos, beyond the cross, *beyond* the old creation. She has never seen it, been in it, nor does she even know it! Yet she was redeemed out of it."

"'Tis beyond me. It is beyond us all."

The Lord turned to speak to his angels.

"What you have seen . . . that girl . . . perfect . . . radiating the full riches of my life . . . and a whole creation destroyed on the cross . . . *that* is what I *always* see. No mortal eyes shall behold these things until *that* day. Nor is it necessary that they behold, for these things you have seen are matters bound neither by time nor eternity. It is not necessary that they behold these things, nor experience them, nor even *believe* them.

"These are matters that *are.* They have been established. Nothing can change that. It is only what I *see* with my eyes, and the things I *know*, because I have visited all ages from beginning to end. Only *these things* are of any import . . . and only these things are *truly* real.

"I *know* what truly *is.*

"Yet, one day, she *shall* see. She shall see herself as I see her . . . as she truly is. And blessed are those who, having not seen, *believe*!"

He paused, looked about, and spoke quietly to himself, "A witness to my resurrection must be made also in realms unseen. But I must come here again before earth's evening. There are eleven men who need me.

"Now," said the Lord in joyful tone, "Now, my everlasting companions . . . *to the throne*!"

Immediately the angels swarmed into the skies, each to his own place . . . creating a great, angelic corridor reaching straight up into the heavenlies.

"To the throne!" they cried.

As natural as it was for him to be on earth, and in a body quite visible, the Lord stepped into thin air and, quite naturally, began to ascend through the midst of that angelic corridor . . . into the sphere of the invisible and the spiritual.

But he would not lay off his earthly vestige as he approached the other realm. A *visible* human being was about to make his home in that quite invisible place.

A *man* in the glory!

He threw one hand high into the air and cried again,

To the throne!

And as angels watched the lowly carpenter step through the portal between two worlds, they saw, for the first time, a man in heavenly realms. They knew they were declaring his rightful place as they cried out in response:

To the throne–
The ever-living One
The triumphant One
The Lamb of God
The carpenter of Nazareth
The Son of Man
The Son of God
The Lord of lords
and
King of kings!

To the throne! To the throne!

THE FINAL ACT

CHAPTER 61

IT IS EVENING. A young woman climbs a high hill, throws back her head, and allows her eyes to wade through the starry sky. Her heart is full of love for a Lord she has worshiped and adored for many years now.

She wonders. On how many occasions, by now, has he stopped time, bypassed eternity, reached back into that primordial era, and, in some mysterious way known only to him, plucked from out of the center of his being . . . *his own life* . . . and thrust that life into the bosom of one who had just believed in him?

How many spirits within the bosom of how many men and women have been raised from the dead and ignited into life? How many souls under transformation? Do eons lie ahead before that last portion of God is implanted in the last believer? Or will it be tomorrow?

When will that vast host of the redeemed be lifted out of time and space to discover for themselves that the cross has put a whole creation to death and made a people wholly righteous? When will they see with *his* eyes? When will they know that the history of the bride began *after* all things?

"When shall we know . . . as we are known," whispers the young woman pensively. She, like her God, has never aged. "Oh, but that is an eternal thing. I am in time!" When will she be freed of these temporal bonds, to *know* these things?

"When . . . shall mortality put on immortality? When . . . shall all inhibitions of the flesh fade away? When . . . will *I* know . . . as he has always known me? When . . . spirit return to Spirit? When . . . his day? When . . . her day?

"When will time and eternity intersect . . . when is *fullness of time*? When shall the bride have made herself ready?

"When shall I cast my eyes into these very skies . . . and see angels . . . ten thousand times ten thousand? Innumerable. Descending! When, earth, will you complete your last orbit . . . and I . . . we . . . be plucked from here by his almighty power? Changed. Before the eyelid can wink. Like him! The veil of the *flesh* broken! *Then* shall I see the unseen. *Then* shall I know as I am known.

"And when the wedding feast?" she seems to ask the stars.

"When shall the fiancée become the bride, and the bride . . . the wife?

"Past, present, future shall dissolve into one, *then* disappear! Then I, as part of that bride, shall love him with all the power and passion of my new being!

"How the consummation?"

She looks again into the skies, from horizon to horizon.

A far-off day begins to fill her mind's eye. She begins to see an event far, far distant . . . even *eternity's last moment.* She begins to see. . . .

CHAPTER 62

WHAT IS THIS EMERGING SCENE? Is it that moment, far past, when God was the All?

No. Yet it is like unto it.

Then what vision is it that we now behold?

A Door opens in the new heavens. A great swarm of light begins to descend from out of that realm. This light, it is a city! The New Jerusalem. A city of a hundred million shining stones, each glowing with the glory of the light that is its center. And the center is the Lord, Christ Jesus!

The city begins its descent, and as it does, it begins to change. A galaxy of living light it is, swirling downward in the skies. Gradually this stardust of light becomes a multitude of people–that vast host of the redeemed, a multitude no man can number.

They are, as one, offering up jubilant praise to their Lord and Savior. The angelic host surrounds them, and together the two hosts join one another in an anthem, unleashing the mightiest tribute of rapturous praise ever to be known.

Around and around their Lord the angels circle, while the vaults of a new heaven and a new earth echo the chants of adulation of redeemed man and elect angels.

The scene begins once more to change.

That vast, innumerable throng standing beneath the angels and before the Lord begins to flow together, becoming, at first, one great light of lights. The brightness grows, the lights become all one. At the center of this light, a form begins to emerge.

The angels exult in holy delight. They recognize that form, for they have seen it once before in a brief moment of glory . . . long ago on the day of his resurrection.

Standing before them is the Bride of the Lamb.

She emerges into clear view, the radiance of her light and glory eclipsing all save the throne of God. She stands before them robed in purity and holiness.

The angels bow with a gentleness and tenderness never before displayed. She is, once more, the reality of the picture. All the loveliness of all womankind is sculptured into one beauty, resting upon her.

An innocence flows from her that enraptures even the holy angels. Her eyes have never seen or known one glimpse of the tragedies that befell the old creation. She stands there in the strength and perfection of youth. Her raven hair, her glowing visage tell a thousand tales of love, of passion, of singular devotion to her Lord. A majesty, a grandeur, and an exalted beauty radiate from her as terrible as the face of God.

For a moment all things else seem to vanish away in the presence of this holy and glorious bride. Suddenly, though, there appears in the distance a yet greater glory.

None else but the King!

The woman begins to glow with a brightness far beyond the ends of belief. The glory of the brightness of the Lord ignites with a fire that immerses–and then consumes–all else. And from within this sea of endless glory . . . arises a shout!

Forever!
No more
alone.

As two gleeful children might, they run toward one another and embrace in an exchange of divine love. With all else having already dissolved, the light of the glory of the two now melts into one.

Long ago the Lord gave up his unconfined endlessness and enfolded himself into that smaller place called eternity. Now, one with his bride, he releases himself back to his true and endless expanse.

Has he, then, become–once more–the All?

Nay, but rather, he has at last become that which he purposed to become, there, before the foundation of the ages. He has become

The All ***in*** *all.*

CHAPTER 63

THE DISTANT VISION BEGINS TO FADE, then it vanishes.

The young woman, now standing at the crest of an emerald hill, rises to her feet, a deep sense of the love of the Lord stirring within her . . . for she has just heard the overwhelming cry of the living Holy Spirit within her.

And that Spirit within her has cried . . . *Come!*

And like Eve before her, she lifts her hands to the skies, raises her voice, believing that her counterpart might hear her . . . and cries:

Come, Lord Jesus. Come!

And just beyond the Door, in realms of glory, he who loves her and died for her . . . now hears her plea.

"At last, she is putting off lesser things, knowledge, service, sacrifice. She is returning to the highest order of the universe.

"She is learning to *love* me," he whispers.

Soon,
yes, soon now . . .
very, very soon . . .

Gabriel!

It is late, and we must say good-bye. I trust you have seen something this hour that will forever remain with you and—perhaps—even change you!

The players, I am told, are preparing another performance. Their first, as you recall, was a drama. Now this, a love story. The next—I hear—shall prove perhaps to be an adventure . . . an adventure into realms unseen. If I am not mistaken, their next production shall be The Chronicles of the Door. Ah! Now there is a tale for the telling. As the Lord wills, I trust we shall meet again, yet thrice.

Book Discussion Guide

1. What was God's purpose in Creation?
2. How is the word *counterparts* used in this book? What would God's counterpart have to be? Do you think it's possible for God to have a counterpart?
3. Can anything about God be "not good"? Does God's aloneness in this story, his yearning for a counterpart, suggest God has needs?
4. Did the creation of woman violate humanity's reflection of God's image (by dividing his oneness)? (Also see Genesis 1:26-28.)
5. In what ways did the original creation of man reflect God's nature and attributes? How do we reflect him today? How has that reflection been distorted?
6. Why do you think God stresses on page 198, "*You*, man, are very much like me"? What is the importance of this distinction? What happens when humans reverse the order, thinking God is very much like us?
7. In this story, God adamantly ended his role as Creator after the six days recorded in Genesis. Is God's work of creation finished?

8. In a few places the author writes that God experienced something by revelation. Can God experience revelation? From where would such a revelation come?

9. What do you think of the author's strong assertion that God has gender, that he is male?

10. In the Genesis account, who notices that it is not good for man to be alone? Why do you think the author chose to show the man realizing this himself?

11. Are giving and receiving love different person to person than person to God? (See pages 223–226.) If so, how do they differ? Why do you think the man in this story was not content with loving and being loved by God? Was God discontent with this exchange?

12. Look at the description of love in chapter 14. How is this similar to love as we experience it today? How does it differ? How can we express love like this?

13. Jesus cited this as the greatest commandment: "You must love the LORD your God with all your heart, all your soul, all your strength, and all your mind" (Luke 10:27). Why is it so difficult for us to wholeheartedly love God?

14. How do we express our love to God? What part of yourself do you hold back? Why? Are service, giving, and worship valid expressions of our love? When are they insufficient?

15. Look at the brief story of Hosea on pages 247–249. Have you ever chosen to love first, even when the other party was wounding you?

16. Do you agree that humanity is imbued with portions of the divine nature? Is God divisible (i.e., can he cordon off portions of himself)? What does the Bible say about this?

17. Reread the passage on page 289 about how Jesus looked at the woman with seven demons. What does he see when he looks at you? into you?

18. Are we "kind of his kind," counterpart to God? Why or why not? What is our relationship to God?

19. What does it mean that creation was crucified with Christ? What practical implications does this have for us?

20. In 2 Corinthians 5:17, we read that "anyone who belongs to Christ has become a new person. The old life is gone; a new life has begun!" What is the nature of this new life? How can we fully live as God created us to be: spiritually? physically?

21. On page 369, the Lord says, "It is only what I *see* with my eyes, and the things I *know* . . . Only *these things* are of any import . . . and only these things are truly real." What does this perspective mean in your life?

About the Author

GENE EDWARDS was born and raised in east Texas, the son of an oilfield roughneck. He graduated from East Texas State University at the age of eighteen, with majors in English literature and English history. His first year of postgraduate work was taken at the Baptist Theological Seminary in Zurich, Switzerland, followed by living in the Holy Lands and then taking up residence in Rome, Italy. He received his master's degree in theology from Southwestern Baptist Theological Seminary in Fort Worth, Texas, at the age of twenty-two. He served as a Southern Baptist minister and then as an evangelist in citywide campaigns sponsored by ministerial alliances.

Gene is the author of more than thirty books, which have been translated into over twenty languages. Some of his books are literary classics, such as *The Divine Romance* and *A Tale of Three Kings.* Today, Gene's ministry includes conferences on the deeper Christian life, as well as raising up gatherings that meet in homes. He and his wife, Helen, make their home in Jacksonville, Florida.

For more information, including a complete list of his works, visit www.geneedwards.com.